"This is a major work of poetry from a writer who has for decades been doing so much more than 'just saying' it. His poems' speakers often figure themselves 'on the outside looking in,' but you get the sense that they know the inside of everything. The poems gracefully know aging. The light their words cast upon us falls but never fails. Such refusal of failure is part of a gentle redefinition of life."

—AL FILREIS, Kelly Professor, University of Pennsylvania

"Stelzig's poems are scholarly and formally adept in equal measure. But their secret weapon is earnestness: they wear their learning lightly, always balancing the intellect with a winning generosity and human tenderness."

—ERICA MCALPINE, Associate Professor of English, University of Oxford

"'I would like to land a poem / the way a boxer lands a blow,' Eugene Stelzig writes in one poem in this rich and varied new collection. I've been reeling from any number of Gene's poems for six decades now. The best poetry sustains us through this life, and Gene's poetry does precisely that, never more so than in this book, where aging and thoughts of death—from the funny to the chilling—begin to dominate and linger."

—ED FOLSOM, Roy J. Carver Professor Emeritus, University of Iowa

"*Just Saying* is the latest volume of lifelong poet and scholar, Eugene Stelzig. Although it covers some of the same ground as his earlier poetry, his approach is fresh and eminently accessible to the casual reader. With wide ranging topics like nature, philosophy, politics, literature, and aging, there is something for everyone to enjoy and relate to."

—ELSJE VAN MUNSTER, Retired Judge

"In meticulously crafted and compassionately humane poems of beguiling intellectual ease and elegance, Eugene Stelzig reminds us that no matter the misery and mayhem we humans inflict on one another and the planet, an infinitely various natural world remains to astonish, comfort and console us. His voice—witty, wise, and seasoned with a lifetime's experience—celebrates with startling clarity the magic of the ordinary amid the doubts and questions that modernity incessantly forces upon us."

—Stephen Behrendt, George Holmes Distinguished University Professor of English Emeritus, University of Nebraska

Just Saying

Just Saying

Selected Poems from My Sixties and Seventies

EUGENE STELZIG

RESOURCE *Publications* • Eugene, Oregon

JUST SAYING
Selected Poems from My Sixties and Seventies

Resource Publications
An Imprint of Wipf and Stock Publishers
199 W. 8th Ave., Suite 3
Eugene, OR 97401

www.wipfandstock.com

PAPERBACK ISBN: 979-8-3852-7252-5
HARDCOVER ISBN: 979-8-3852-7253-2
EBOOK ISBN: 979-8-3852-7254-9

VERSION NUMBER 02/26/26

Contents

TRACES

Contents

Contents

WHERE THE LIGHT FALLS

SOME THINGS

Contents

EPHEMERAL EFFUSIONS OF AN AGING BRAIN DURING PANDEMIC TIMES

Acknowledgments

The author gratefully acknowledges the following publications in which these poems have previously appeared:

"On Seeing Two Women in a Passionate Embrace," *ImageOutWrite*,

"Joe the Lost Poet," *Mo' Jo The Anthology*,

"Things Unthinkable," *Trumped: A Poets Anthology*,

"Mr. Jones," *Walls: A Poets Anthology*,

"All Our Ships Have Sailed," *The Penn Review*.

"Ingolstadt," "What Is," "At a Baroque Concert," "Golden October Days," "The Inward Path," "Zarathustra's Song" in *Le Mot Juste* [the annual anthology of Rochester Just Poets organization].

Traces

But if we look into the bulk of our species, they are such as are not likely to be remembered a moment after their disappearance. They leave behind them no traces of their existence, but are forgotten as though they had never been.

Joseph Addison, *Spectator* 16, March 4, 1712

FOR BENJAMIN ROBERT HAYDON

You spent your tumultuous life
in an unremitting passion
for grandiose history painting
on canvases stretched large enough
to suit your outsized ego
in the pursuit of High Art.

The Elgin marbles you first recognized
for their authentic Phidian splendor.
In a solitary vigil you conned them
during cold nights by candlelight.
Their antique anatomies idealized in
frozen stone you championed against
a skeptical art establishment.
The functionaries of the Royal Academy
you called out in flaming print for
hanging your Dentatus canvas in the shade.

You were keen to paint the modest
Wellesley, victorious at Waterloo,
but saw the defeated emperor as
your alter ego in his meteoric
trajectory. Wordsworth and Keats
you boldly planted in the scene of the
Judean's entry into Jerusalem: they
were your friends and recognized in you
a compatriot of their aspiring selves.

In the poet laureate brooding on top
of Mount Helvellyn you saw yourself.

In and out of debtor's prison in your
later years, you soldiered on teaching
the next generation the fundamentals
of design. Harassed by creditors you
crooked your knee in the parlors of the
titled, and shrunk down to the profitable
portrait trade whose subjects you drew well
but despised as unfit for your heroic brush.

When hope gave out and the creditors
closed in, you adapted a line from King
Lear as you put a bullet in your head,
spraying blood on canvas as your last
word. When that bullet failed to finish
you, you took up a razor and cut your
throat. Your body you managed to kill,
but not the shining.

WHEN I CONSIDER

When I consider our universe now thought
to be some fourteen billion years old,
and that mysterious Big Bang that as we are told
has given rise to that infinite lot
of billions of celestial cities known
as galaxies forever moving out
in space and time, and when I read about
mysterious Black Holes and Dark Matter I own
I'm at a loss to know who or what we
are. I think as we slowly begin to see
more and more of this strange world we've been shown
by the learned astronomers the less
we have a clue even how to guess
why we are here in this vast cosmos all alone.

TRACES

Nobody should have to live
without leaving some trace
on the palimpsest of life.

Faces disappear like leaves
or empires but every face
is one of a kind;
a spirit sword raised
against the void.

To leave a mark is our
proper privilege, whether
in word, deed, pigment,
stone, print, or even a
a single gesture seared
in someone's soul.

TIME

We ride a fast
moving wave
advancing toward
an unknown shore
whose crest we surf
hoping not to wipe out
before we complete
a flawless run

HIDDEN LIFE

The mist-shrouded September fields suffused
by the early morning sun
speak of it
and so does the flaming orange-tinted light
filtering through the crepuscular trees.

The late afternoon sun so
translucent
that floods my mouth and ears
speaks of it
as do the speckled leaves
drifting in the sighing breeze.

All things that are out of doors this day
bask in the brimful but unseen presence
of that hidden life
deep down everything.

REVENANTS

Year after year they return
those red-breasted robins
who build their nests
on the solid crossbeam
underneath our deck
facing the Genesee Valley
and the afternoon sun.
At first we knocked them
down at summer's end
but now we leave the nests
to front the winter winds,
season after season.

By late March or early April
the pairs are back, traipsing around
on our front lawn with a casual
insouciance as if we were
the visitors and they the
permanent residents who
tolerate our presence.

Their nests are bursting at least
twice during the summer
with wide-mouthed offspring
gaping at the sky and
demanding constant nurture
from harried parents.

Later we see the fledglings
flounder in the warm air
as they hazard their hapless
and abortive first flights.

By late summer or early
September they have all fled
their nests now so bare and stark
against the fading light
of diminished days.

APRIL 19, 2008

Only two weeks ago
it was bitter cold,
snow still checkering the ground,
heaped and crusted drifts on the side
of the road, and the teeth-chattering
winds blasting up the valley's slope.
Suddenly yesterday the temperature
rose all the way to eighty, and today
it hit eighty-six, setting a new record.

Has Nature run temporarily amok
or is this a dramatic harbinger
of the prophesied blast furnace
of global warming here in the first
decade of the new millennium?

Rocketing from mid-winter to mid-
summer in two weeks is a wild
roller coaster ride into an
uncertain future that only
the reckless can relish.

GIVE IT A BREAK

I listen to the evening news
and wonder how the world can have
gone on so long with the way we
humans have been carrying on in
our inimitable ways for untold
millennia. Always there are
several wars on different continents,
as well as fires, floods, quakes, and
storms that beggar description.
The victim counts and death tolls
accumulate over the decades to
unimaginable proportions. We do
unto each other, and nature does
unto us, and even more so we
do unto nature.

Yet despite all wars,
diseases, and natural disasters,
not to mention the steady toll
of traffic fatalities, day after day
the human population proliferates.
We encumber the earth, crowd out,
enslave or exterminate other species.

This planet deserves a rest or a
reprieve from us and our horrendous
ways, if only to regain its balance,
heal its wounds, recover its green
prehuman song in a fertile world
without the noise of jet engines,
automobiles, cell phones, radios,
televisions, gunfire, or even the
faintest trace of any human voice.

The good earth needs a break from us.

ESCAPEE POEM

I think of one of those poems
I nearly held in my hands
and that like a bird
long watched and waited for
suddenly flew away
just as my hands were about
to close upon it.

What branch or whose brain
do they now grace
and tease with their allure?
What bait can bring
them back into
my dreaming soul?

MOUNTAIN STREAMS AND BUTTER

When I was a boy in that *Sound-of-*
Music Austrian town nestled between
the high Alps, you used to come once
a week around lunchtime from a
nearby village and deliver farm-
fresh eggs and butter the size
of a bowling ball wrapped in
a cool moist cloth. My father
would sit with you in the kitchen
trading jokes and stories
swathed in a blue nimbus of
unfiltered cigarette smoke.

A half century later I went back
to Austria with my older sister to visit
you in the retirement home. Now
blind and nearly deaf in your late
nineties, you lovingly traced her
face with your fingers, softly
feeling your way at a snail's
pace. Everything about you
now was haltingly slow, even
your replies to our questions.
Your senses were failing,
but your mind was still there.
After a long pause you stated
softly, but with deep conviction,

Alles ist vergänglich:
Everything is transitory.

Sybil-like you pronounced the
sum of your long life's experience
with rock-solid conviction.
Soon after when word reached us
that you had died I thought
of eggs, mountain streams, and butter.

DOGGEREL AT SIXTY-FIVE

When you realize you're about to turn sixty-five
it gets harder to keep hope alive.
The extraction of a long-decayed tooth
fills your mind with ruth.

You still have plenty of hair
but you're also eligible for Medicare.
True, it's turned mostly grey, but it
looks like you'll keep it for many a day.

Your body's aches do not your mind delight.
At sixty-five you may not be up to the fight
against the slow onset of ageing's blight.

You have no choice but to soldier on
and make the best of what wears on the bone.
Exempt from this general scourge there are none.

You keep your fingers crossed and count your days.
What bullets are coming you hope to dodge.
Fortuna that fickle wench has her nasty ways,
you pray that none of these with you will lodge.

You harvest your thoughts and watch the seasons.
You wait for the blue heron to land on your pond.
You're too old to live your life by mere reasons
and not yet old enough not to be fond
of far-fetched dreams and foolish fantasies
that prey on your mind with the weight of disease.

Mostly you're glad to take your days as they come
and with which you feel comfortably at home.
Your kind spouse keeps you from feeling alone.

At sixty-five you hope your life is far from done
but you know from the death of friends long gone
that the Great Harvester can always be counted on.

SECOND SKIN

In the wooded paths I have
to myself I absorb the deep
forces of the earth through
the soles of my feet. I
put my hands on the trunk
of a massive, aged tree
to feel its enormous power
course through me. My
eyes, nose, mouth, and
ears take in the primeval
world as I walk lost
in my own thoughts,
immersed in my
second skin.

NOTHING OTHER THAN ITSELF

(an answer to Percy Shelley)

Slowly they spin, twist,
twirl, swirl to the ground.
They float on the air like
butterflies, they wing the wind
like birds. They ride
the air, descending one by one,
dropping, veering, swerving,
each falling from
the denuding branches
in a cascade of many
hues, an exfoliated palette
checkering the ground,
their motion spent,
entropic bier of the
turning season, seedbed
of a world to come,
perpetual circle or cycle
in the play of the elements
that is nothing other than its
irrefrangible material self.

LAMENT FOR THE MAKARIS

I weep for Jimi Hendrix
The cat is gone before his prime
O weep for Jimi Hendrix!
Who would not weep for him
He knew himself to sing
And play upon the rock guitar
Thundering from star to star

You first blazed across the television screen
In Merrie England's Top of the Pops
With your filed teeth
Hippy flowerchild freak
Plucking the strings
Until your electric guitar
Caught on fire and
You were launched:
The Jimi Hendrix Experience

O American Dionysus sunflower
Acid tripping turned on man
Antihero hellfire satyr
Rock voyant and fleur du mal

Hey Joe! Shot up shot down
Where you gonna run to now?

At Woodstock the Starspangledbanner
You stretched out like a rubber band
In cosmic slow motion
Anthem For Doomed Youth
Electrovaulted over stampeded fields of mud
Dancing enraptured naked slimecreatures
And threedays' worth of accumulated trash

Galaxy hopping inimitable Jimi
Who like a mad dog on his own
Vomit gagging in Londontown
Drowned. Are You Expeeeerienced?

I weep for Jimi whose flaming
Guitar chords still sound
The world over all along the watchtowers
Still pulling in money
For the gods of the marketplace
Still caressing his guitar
With his teeth
Still high as a kite
On an invisible string
Surfing the stratosphere:
Scuse me while I kiss the sky.

O weep for Jimi Hendrix
The cat is gone
Dead in his prime
He had his life as in his time

And knew himself to sing and sound
The electric Zarathustra feedback chorus
Of the Sixties rock guitar

Thundering from star to star

(1970, revised 2008)

NOVEMBER 5, 2008 (OBAMA ELECTED)

Sometimes in the darkest hour
we can see the wheel of history
turn in the right direction.
Yesterday it did, and we
we were there to see its
myriad radiant arcs cast
by its spokes across the globe.
We were there. Oh yes we were.

CORDELIA IN DOVER

I have come to these white cliffs and to this
heath simply from the need of the heart to
relieve the misery of a serpent-stung
and weed-bedecked parent too mortified
to partake of the help I offer with
open arms and no ulterior motive
of military conquest or dynastic
succession. Great France has offered his
power to do what is only right for
an abused king and father who has run
from me and mine and hides him in the wheat.

What balm can soothe that battered heart, what
hope restore that tempest-fretted frame to
any semblance of sanity and sounder days?
O search him out in the fields shrouded in
Channel mists, bring him to me, the banished
one come to restore him to his rightful self,
to bless him with the simplest and most cordial
of all gifts: my love, and nothing but my love.

OPHELIA'S WET DREAM

I am a swan in a world of my own
simply letting myself float
in this warm and limpid liquid
far away from my prying father's eyes
and my hectoring brother's tongue.
With my long spindrift hair I slowly
glide downstream, my gown spread
wide like a white sail on the surge,
far away from the mother I never knew
and the mercurial soliloquizing lover
who berated and abandoned me for doing
my prolix father's and that bloated
lecherous alcoholic ass the new king's
bidding.
            I am borne away from these
who have betrayed me, immersed in my
own aqueous element, my sweet moist
nothing untouched, my water fantasies
quietly unfolding with the current
of that soft and welcoming flood
bearing me on and on I know not where.

IAGO

I swore by two-faced Janus,
I was the ensign who threw out
a false regimental flag.
Don't ask me any questions
as to why I did
what I did.
I did what I did and
you know what you know.

The swaggering thick-lips with
his African tall tales
and his young Venetian piece
with her mincing show
of infatuated innocence
deserved no better than
what I dished out to them.

I will tell you nothing
even if you tear me
limb from limb.
Life's a game of chess
and I was always at least
two moves ahead of everyone.
I always enjoyed playing
a devious role and
never condescended to
wear my heart on my sleeve.

My exquisite delight
was that I fooled
everyone even if I
alone could appreciate
the consummate craftsmanship
of my infernal knavery.

I was always acting for
an audience of one
laughing at my own joke.

THE MELANCHOLY DANE (TAKE ONE)

I've come to be known as the prince of the
soliloquy, sounding off about being
or not being yet not ever having really
lived my life in any fashion to suit my
lofty words. They say I could talk a
good game, but when it came to deeds
I was the Great No Show. True, I was adept
at skewering the fools, sycophants and
schemers at court with scalpel-sharp words
they mostly could not fathom ("very like a
whale"). Words were my weapons, and I
wielded them to the hilt with a self-delighting
sarcasm ("Go seek him there yourself")
or salacious raillery ("a fair thought to lie
between a Maid's legs"). A sometime
playwright I also knew how to wake a
crowned killer's sleeping conscience
and have him feel the sting of bitter words
aimed dead on at his coruscated soul.

I had my triumph when he ran from the theater
in sheer panic and when I shadowed him
in the prayer he knew could not expunge
his fratricidal crime nor the guilty
indulgences of his incestuous sheets.

Stabbing him with the tainted sword contrived
by him and forcing him to drink the poison
tempered by his own hand was sweet revenge
even if it came with my expiring breaths.

Was this not a satisfying show and
more than mere words? Was this not a deed done
to right the ship of state? I acted on impulse
but knew exactly what I was doing unlike
when I stabbed behind the curtain and
dispatched that rash intruding fool. That
officious ass stuck his meddling nose
where it oughtn't to have been and got his
well-deserved comeuppance. As did my
old school friends who tried to play me
like a pipe but lost their heads instead.
Thanks, Great England, ha ha ha. I did a
deed, and then some, no mere word monger me.

I performed some purging of a corrupt world
even as I was about to leave its stage.
Pleased I was with what I'd done, content to
depart this unpromising and fallen scene
nor needing my stoic friend's, Horatio's,
uncharacteristically sentimental "may
flights of angels" etcetera to send me
on my way. As for the rest, I neither
know nor care if it's silence so long as
I'm away from these perpetual fools.

HAMLET (TAKE TWO)

The hypertrophy of cogitation: yes,
thinking too precisely on the event,
reading in the book of my own soul
has become the signature of my name.
Cheap Plaster of Paris is all that is.
They slander me in a misprision most
severe, for if anything I underthought
the very issues in play, lost at sea,
amazed, dazed, appalled by all I heard or
thought I saw for the first time, the film
fallen from my eyes: the brute, the carnal,
the crass and the grasping. Stunned, staggered
I was when the old King came hot to trot
for revenge. Claudius of course I knew
for a slimebag, a rank goat, but my
mother's fall set my senses reeling at
the spectacle of Mr. Garbage bedding
with the Queen. From Purgatory then the old
warrior came, bloated with self-pity, hellbent
on a quid pro quo for his horned head,
insistent that I dispatch this lecherous
sliver of our blood. Maybe I should have thought
to call the octogenarian to account for
demanding that blood instead of heeding
our Lord's gospel message on which he should
have had plenty of time to reflect in the place

of his flaming confinement. Maybe I
should have asked him why his loving queen
fell away from Hyperion him into
the arms of a carousing satyr. Why
had he not noticed the change? Why had he
not paid her any heed? And why had he
not thought of the consequences of asking
for such polluted blood? Had he not considered
how this revenge might taint his son and
in the end put the son of his slain foe,
young Fortinbras, on the throne of Denmark?
And had I fully thought through what he failed
to process in the fever of his ghostly fit, I
might have saved the very kingdom and myself.

THE CHANDOS SHAKESPEARE

(National Portrait Gallery, London, August 2009)

For half an hour and more you contemplate
this portrait pregnant with psychic power
while the tourists pause, then traipse on by.
You stare at the long black gypsy hair,
the rakish earring, the globed forehead
that intimates a world of its own making.
You wonder at that riveting mysterious
face's surprising transformations
in your spellbound dreaming mind.
The longer you look the more its shifting
features fascinate and confound.
It surely is the face of one who knew his kind,
but is this painting's the genuine face
of the Stratford poet, or is it that
of some other, lesser, unknown man?
For a timeless instant you stand in awe
worrying that question for an answer
to satisfy a craving built up over
decades of teaching the plays that have
enchanted the world for four plus centuries
with Prosper's potent charms. Is this the face
of that mysterious master impresario
who has earned the world's applause
and whose life so long ago melted
into thin air? Is this *his* face?

You pause and look again, you take in that
face until it becomes a part of your self
even as its features begin to dematerialize:
all but the lips, slightly curled in the hint
of an ironic smile, and then the eyes
so all-knowing that they mesmerize.
The longer you gaze into those dark
vessels of pooled light shining so serene
you see that they are the very eyes
of the man who saw through the whole
human spectacle with a vision keen
and worked his magic to coin it into
words before that great sleep we all must share
put an untimely end to him, but not to them.

BEYOND THE REACHES OF OUR SOULS

When the autumn winds blow the sodden leaves
across the weather-beaten fields they stir
thoughts beyond the reaches of our souls.

When this ancient earth quakes and heaves
and thousands lose their lives in a cataclysmic
sequence of flood and fire thoughts beyond
the reaches of our souls flounder in the void

where no answer is to questions that might
make up our sum. Only the stars glitter
in the cold remoteness of deep space

as we ask and ask of some Beyond where our
reachings cannot reach. Wretched as we are
in the whir and blur of our fleeting lives

we cannot help but puzzle over those inchoate
thoughts beyond the reaches of our souls
that make us wonder who and what we are.

EGO

You can sell
the power of the wind,
you can conserve
the shine
of the sun

You can feed your face full
and spare not a crumb
for anyone

You can take and take
and leave only the ache
of utter emptiness

You can make yourself
the perpetual
Number one

In your universe
and care less
about the cost
of what others have lost

You can add up
what you've earned
with your gilded greed

At the expense of others'
need
while you ignore
their pain

But remember
that with all
you've gained
you can never give
away the rain
and that despite all
you have won
you never can
own the sun.

THE PERFECT TERRORIST (HAITI, JANUARY 2010)

A dusty black arm reaches skyward from
a heap of rubble, the hand with spread
digits rigid in rigor mortis, one victim
of some two hundred thousand buried
alive or shaken to death in a moment
in a cataclysm of broken, twisted
limbs and blood, collapsed buildings now
fodder for feasting rats and bulldozers.

Osama, eat out your frozen heart, if you
can find it, and remember this:
nature is the perfect terrorist.

GOODBYE

We live
day to day,
and the days come
and then they go
like the leaves on the trees
and the clouds in the sky

We see
friends we have known
become strangers
and fade from our lives

We feel
the seconds, minutes, and hours
run through our hands
like water
that we can't hold

We watch
them go
and even as we grow
old
we still don't know
that we're always
saying goodbye.

ICICLES IN MOONLIGHT (FEBRUARY 2010)

Gleaming spears of advancing winter's
lustrous progress suspended from
eaves weighed down by snow, polished
by the crystalline moonlit nights
encroaching upon the shortening days

Little do you know that all too soon
the melting sun of the advancing spring
will eat away and diminish you
growing shorter as the days grow long
until slow drip by slow drop
you will disappear without leaving a trace
of where or what you once were.

VESPA DREAM

Now in your sixties you still
dream of that shiny red motor
scooter you rode with such glee
in college a lifetime ago with
the wind in your face on your
way to a jazz club, a folk
festival, or a bar somewhere
or other with a dark-haired
girl astride behind you riding
the wet streets of West Philly
on a rainy day as you slide on
the slippery cobble stones and
steel trolley tracks and you
both laugh with wild glee.

You see your young self
kick-starting the motor and
shifting those gears on the
handlebar, letting out the
clutch with such ease and
riding so free, flying on a
sheer cushion of air.

GOING

I do not know where I am going
but I find my way
by going as I go.

There is no map, no compass,
no calendar, no chart,
no end in sight

Though I know
there is an end
to the going.

I do not know where I am going
but I find my way
by going as I go.

In wind and rain and sun and snow
I go not knowing
where I go.

Although the way is long
and the end
toward which we go
unknown

We cannot be lost
because we find our way
by going as we go.

CALLIMACHUS KNEW

Callimachus knew what the ancient
Chinese poets also knew:
the fewer the words
the better
especially when dealing
with the Big Subjects.

Callimachus knew that
the rain and the sunshine
are always there
and best left to speak
for themselves.

Callimachus knew that the echoes
of other poets are
a cacophony to
the genuine voices
from within.

Let them speak in few,
let them abide in the silence.

Callimachus knew.

SILENT REVERY

I stand in the wood
by the fern-dappled brook
and listen to the soothing
sound of water washing
over stones polished smooth
by that unending flood.

I shut my eyes to take
in the plashy murmur
that already was before
our kind came into being.

With eyes closed I thrill
to the pure essence of
water flowing through
the mind until the whine
of a jetliner far overhead
startles me out of my
solitary and silent revery.

LATE SUMMER

The shrill vibrato of the unseen cicadas
rises to a crescendo and then suddenly dies.
The cawing of the crows resounds in the cornfield.
The humid cloud-drifted skies of late afternoon
settle in the mind like a wet blanket.
Underneath all the other sounds there is
the crickets' and the grasshoppers' unending choir.
The sun-long days grow steadily shorter
and the weight of the heat lifts only at night.
Dawn's cooling breezes stir the flowers and ferns.
Summer seems eternal, and autumn so far away.
Its unheard harbinger is the occasional
fall of a single yellowed leaf on the green lawn.
The horse chestnuts are still ripening on the trees.

BROKEN PROMISES

We make and then break
promises we mean to keep.
We try to change our spots
but during our sleep they
resume their old forms
like cicatrices that mark
our skin. Wish as we
will, try as we might
they abide with us
when we wake.

We cannot alter
the signature of self
indelibly imprinted
in the very fabric
of our being.

Its deep dye
is most visible
in those moments
when we seek to deny
who or what we are.
We are who we are.
We have failed our promises,
or they have failed us,
but we remain the same.

JESUS IN WEST HOLLYWOOD

Plucked from their downtown hotels
the polyglot tourists gather at
the Starline terminal waiting
for their six-hour Grand Tour
of Greater Los Angeles to see the
Hollywood Sign and the Hollywood
Bowl and Beverly Hills and Rodeo
Drive and the Walk of Fame and
the Kodak Theater and Sunset
Strip and so Much More.

As they wait for their tour bus
and guide a street person approaches
and parks himself at the bottom of the
terminal steps. With shoulder-length
locks of luxuriant black hair and
a ragged coat this thirty-something
stranger talks animatedly to himself,
gesticulating with his pale hands.

By some unspoken convention the
stranger is ignored by the tourists and
and the Starline staff. No one stares
at him or makes eye contact. No one
cares as his hands move on their
own, orchestrating the babble of
his lips. Is he conducting the music
of the distant stars, or the flight of
of the birds across continents,
or is it the city's freeway traffic
his hands regulate?

No one pays him any
heed; his unheard words have no purchase
on anything or anyone surrounding
him on this raw Sunday morning:
Jesus preaching in West Hollywood.

FALLEN WORLD

All my life long lost
in the primordial cave
I have sought the trace
of some other realm
still present in
our fallen world:

The leaf in the wind,
the flight of the bird,
the cloud's drift,
the brook's flow.

The mind's imprint
in the material world
tracking itself,
that elusive trace
of being's ground
now here, now there
everywhere and nowhere.

DECEMBER BLISS

Entwined in each other's arms
here we lie in our cozy bed
on a cold December day.

In the bliss of our mutual presence
and in the miracle of close touch
we feel that we are one.

Although we know that death
will seek to sunder us
some distant day,

for now we simply lie here
and dream the time away
in the pearled peace
of our togetherness.

PEBBLES [FOR BILL RUECKERT]

A wise man once told me
that writing a book is like
throwing a pebble into
the Grand Canyon.
Over the years I have thrown
several such pebbles.

And oh yes what a
grand canyon it is,
and oh what joy
to have tossed some
pebbles into it.

THE GOLDEN TRACK
[FOR HERMANN HESSE]

on the lowest rung of Jacob's ladder
he sat listening
beyond the horizon

to a most ancient melody.

in a certain mood he thought
that music comes closest to

the golden track of the Immortals.

he never even caught a glimpse of it
but at certain privileged moments
he had let us say intimations

of the fringe of an angel's skirt
tickling his brain
like a transcendental feather duster.

yes maybe music does come closest to
those golden galaxies

whose radiant syntax is forever
beyond our mere deciphering.

Whistling in the Wind

DYING FLAMES

Even as we see others' flames gutter out
we cannot fathom that we will suffer
a similar fate. We assume rather
that we're not subject to the same cruel rout
that sweeps the multitude from life's bright stage.
Even as the years pass and silent age
steals up on us we know not what we're about.
We think our little light will beat the odds.
We carry on like our lives have no term
and that we have the endurance of the gods
who preside above the seasons like the stars.
But deep down in our very bones we know
that what makes us in the end also mars
us and drops the curtain on our too-brief show.

WHALE SONGS

Did the first angels of the antique world
hear those mysterious sounds of the deep blue
and wonder if they were a terrestrial echo
of the music of the spheres? Such cerulean
sonic booms constitute a magisterial symphony
subtending our world. Those giant baritones
of the seas still sound in our blood
if we have spirit ears to hear shut-eyed
the resonating calls from the primeval depths
that sustain the floating continents
on the sleek backs of those gargantuan
dancers of the deep gliding so far below
signaling to each other in the silent seas,
sounding the calls of their ancient world.

WHISTLING IN THE WIND

All his long life he had whistled in the wind.
His wayward notes blew back against his face
like wet leaves. His lame attempts never found
a resonance, yet he kept on resolutely
blowing refractory tunes through pursed lips.
Perhaps there was a secret melody there
that none could hear. Perhaps the scattered
fragments of sound found their harmony
in some other world tuned to a different key.
Perhaps his whistling in the wind realized
there its proper form and found a home.
Or could it be that the act of simply whistling
was all the satisfaction that he ever sought
for the silent song sounding in his heart?

ALZHEIMER'S (FOR A FRIEND)

At first smidgeons or shards of darkness
like crows rising in a distant field
striated the furthest edges of his consciousness.

Much later tides of absence
and lagoons of the unrecoverable
began to flood the landscape of the familiar
under a perpetually setting sun.

The distant horizon grew fainter and fainter
and slowly faded away into the silence of night.
And then the deep dark of the eternal sea
folded into itself even the faintest trace
of any residual memory.

HABIT OR HEBETUDE?

Is it habit or merely hebetude that
makes me sit so still on the
massive trunk of this fallen tree
and watch the noontime sunlight
filtering through the bright curtain
of late spring leaves sheltering
me under broad branches in
this lush green retreat listening
to the intermittent calls of birds
whose names I do not know?

Is it that I feel grounded here
in this leaf-screened harbor so far
removed from the traffic of the world?
Is it because here I can come home
to myself even as I take in the
hidden life pulsing all around me?

STRANGE

Strange it is
how we remember
and do not remember

scenes from our childhood
that far-away country
where people speak

a foreign idiom
we once knew
like the inside of our mouth

but that is now as unfamiliar
as a crater on the moon
of a distant star

in another galaxy
where we were once
quite at home

with our native tongue.

OLD MEN

He was watching the pure lineaments of the sky
when a group of young women in tight shorts walked by.
Being old he knew that only the beauty of the mind endures,
and that beauty of the flesh is as fleeting as summer rain.
But being old he also knew that no matter how true
the former, old men prefer the latter time and again
when it emerges so suddenly out of the blue.

A FEW THINGS OLD MEN KNOW

What you aspired to in your youth
will come back to haunt you
in your later years.

A kindness you performed unthinkingly
may someday pay rich dividends.

Those who insist too righteously on justice
usually harbor bloody thoughts
in their hearts.

Hold on to something too tight
and you break it;
hold it too loose
And you will lose it.

There's no quicker way to fail
than after sudden success.

Sooner or later too much
officiousness, no matter
how apparently in control
of the day, will break
its own neck.

Sometimes even as one door closes
another opens so long as
you let the one door close
and don't expect another to open.

The longer you live
the more you realize that
the deep structure of the world
imitates the deep structure of
Shakespeare's plays.

Those who cry out too much
against public corruption may
have designs on your wallet.

The young have their hopes,
the old their memories.

ON SEEING TWO WOMEN IN A PASSIONATE EMBRACE (OXFORD, JULY 2012)

Oh let them love
if love it is
for love is bliss,

Oh let them kiss
in a passionate embrace,
and let them give
each other's all,

For love even after the Fall
is paradisiacal.

Oh let them love
and hold each other dear
so tender and so near

And let them prove
in their entwined togetherness
that the bonds of true love

Reach far beyond
the mere material contingencies
of womb and tomb.

CALIBAN ABANDONED

This island's all mine own again
with its haunting melodies of wind and rain.
Prospero's taken his books and his daughter
and left me here to fend for myself.
I coveted both when I served his whims,
his books for the potent spells they contained,
and Miranda to people this isle with little Calibans.

At night I still hear strange sounds
that charm my ears and make me forget
the pregnant hag who littered me here.
I was taught to name the greater
and the lesser lights that shine by day and night
by the usurper I sought to kill for forcing me
to do his bidding. Alone again I have come
to realize that the only freedom is that
of the mind. Impatient and domineering
as he was he didn't think that I could learn.
Little faith had he, and gave me less credit.

But learn through his tutelage I did, though
what good this knowledge can do me
in the wake of his departure I have
yet to discover as I attend to the
strange sounds that play about
my ears and make me wonder

exactly who and where I am in
my complete and utter abandonment.

OXFORD LEAVE-TAKING (AUGUST 20, 2012)

On my last day here
after six summers of teaching
the exuberant young
I watch three white doves perched atop
a spire rising high above the chapel
into a pure blue evening sky
in the Harry Potter cloisters
of New College.

Forty-four years ago I bid
a similar farewell to Cambridge
on my last day
as a student at King's College
mesmerized by the roses
of Great Saint Mary's that seemed
to impart a message to my soul
of the enduring beauty
of the mind present there
for untold centuries.

This glorious evening too is
privileged. There is the cooing
of the pigeons, the tolling of
the seven o'clock bells,
and then the quiet of the
green lawns and flower beds

in the college garden where
I take the full measure of this
place that seems momentarily
suspended in time.

The medieval monks who
cultivated the arts of thought
and prayer in these ghostly cloisters
must have known the peace
that passes understanding.

This fabled place so haunted
by the past and not immune
to the blood spilled by the passing
generations is yet an island of peace
in a time full of noise and the riot
of competing claims that leave
their daily scars on the body of
a dangerous and troubled world.

But here in the silence of stone and flower
I know that there is respite for
those who cultivate the quiet
of the concentrated soul

And that even as our little lives
are fretted and frittered away
in the pedestrian fever of the day
there yet is a realm of
things that endure.

On this charmed and serene August
evening of white doves and blue skies
I know in my aging bones that
this is and will always be so in
our relentlessly driven lives
where there is so little time
for the reflective pauses of
the contemplating mind.

SPECIAL OCCASION

In the pressing heat of late summer
I harvested them in an old bucket
with mosquitoes buzzing around
me and my hands scratched by
thorns and brambles as I pushed
my way through thickets to reach
the rich shiny black clusters of
ripe berries. After sweaty hours
on the hunt, I trudged back home
in triumph. You washed the berries
before packing them in plastic
bags to be put in the freezer.

The first richly moist bunch
was a tart dessert piquant
on our eager tongues. I
insisted that we have the frozen
ones only on rare and special
occasions. Untouched they lay
for years in a deep freeze,
forgotten and forlorn.

When you cleaned out the freezer
you wanted to toss the bags
in the garbage because you
were sure the berries had spoiled.

But stubborn I said no,
let's defrost them because
I bet they're still okay. They
were sort of, but had lost all
their taste, wet and bland
rain berries in our mouths.
I took the remaining bags
and threw them in the trash.

That was the special occasion
we had saved them for
all these frozen years.

FOR TOWNES VAN ZANDT (1944–97)

Nike-like your poet's soul has taken
wing on flying shoes. I think of you
somewhere out there in the trackless
wilds on the run with Pancho and Lefty.

Outlaw rambling guitar playing bard
your sad songs I hear sounding in
the wind and the rain and the
river whose voices you recorded
in your haunting melodies.

Footloose star gazer, wind stalker,
even as you sought to soothe your pain
you found your way to an untimely
grave. Sainted singer lost in the
labyrinth of our dark world,
your voice now is
free to the elements.

FATHER OF THE MAN

"the Child is Father of the Man"

My father-of-the-man
sky was wide open then,
the horizon far away.

The blank slate of my child self bore no
burdens troubling my mind
other than the doings
of the day.

The past was an invisible cloud
hanging over me
quite unaware.

My shadow unseen by me, I
carried the ancestral signature of my
genes without the pull of any
temporal gravity.

I did not know,
I did not need to know,
I did not care to know
that the neural network of my mind
was written in the blood of generations.

That my future might consummate
their secret dreams.
That my failures might damn,
my successes indemnify
them.

I did not know
that whatever I would do
or could do or wish to do
was simply a variation on a theme
or a repetition in a different key.

I did not care
that my life was a reprint
of an old book based
on an ancient manuscript
written in the language of the stars.

I did not know that whatever
I would choose to do had
been done uncounted times
before, would be done unnumbered
times more.

I did not know,
I did not care to know.

QUIET AS A MOUSE

Quiet as a mouse Virginia Woolf
left her house and walked into
the River Ouse at the age of fifty-nine.
She put her walking stick on the ground
and looked around for heavy stones
to put in her coat pocket
to weigh her down for good.
Days later her stick was found
by the riverbank and those
who knew her guessed the rest.

What was she thinking as she
walked into this liquid underworld?
Did she assume she was one
of Ophelia's daughters
seeking a room of her own
as she sank under the water
to be bedded in an oozy grave?

Did she believe this was her last will
and testament written in the wet element?
Was she seeking to seal her own legend
with her last breath, or was her
sinking death simply the inevitable
final act of a lifelong struggle
against despair?

PERPLEXITY

The raw perplexity of our being
fell upon me as I walked in the wood
and the naked wonder of our seeing.

Lost in the fog of our self-seeking
none of us can glimpse the sky of our own good
in the raw perplexity of our being.

I've hunted trails that led to no clearing,
no compass had I, no water, no food,
only the naked wonder of our seeing.

Some pilgrim souls forge paths of their own making,
and some lost in the labyrinth know they should
face the raw perplexity of their being.

Some soldier on in the dark with hearts aching,
and some know they would be happy if they could
feel the naked wonder of our seeing.

I should walk in the wood by way of freeing
me from the world's bias if only I could
face the raw perplexity of our being
and the naked wonder of our seeing.

LITTLE THINGS

Late in life I've found my place
in Littleness.
After the Big Dreams of my youth
have fizzled out
the Little has become the order
of my day. Of the many books I've read
I've barely retained a smidgeon
and I've gained even less knowledge
of the refractory human heart.

So much aspiration, so much
effort and anxiety,
and pray tell for what?
I've found now that it's the Little things
that ground my being
and anchor me in this
perplexing world.

The sound of birds in the wood,
of water gurgling in the brook,
of the wind in the trees
is what I've come to count on.

The stone slabs I lug home
from the brook bed feel most
real to me as their gravity

pulls on my knees, shoulders,
and back, signifiers of the material
world we take for granted.

It's these Little Things I've come
to appreciate, and I leave the Big
to those who still aspire.
The Little is where I'm at.

ONCE AGAIN IN NEW COLLEGE GARDEN (OXFORD, JULY 15, 2013)

Here I sit on an old bench
observing a yellow butterfly
flutter by as some large
blue birds wing their silent
way from branch to branch
of a colossal tree, and the pigeons
are perched and cooing on
the ancient city wall.

They go about their business
not heeding in the least my
observant human self.
Their lives no doubt are
short and fleeting, but they
don't seem to mind.

A millennium amounting to
to some thirty human lifetimes
is fleeting too, less than
nothing even, in the grand
cosmic scheme of things.

All those lives come and
gone, coming and going,
year after year, and here
I sit in silent thought

taking in the doings of these
mysterious creatures who in
their own way may well know
what we humans forever fail
to process in all the opacity
of our conscious being.

JOE THE LOST POET

In 1798 there actually were three who teamed up
in the vein of lyrical balladry: Will (Wordsworth),
Sam (Coleridge), and Joe. But just as Pete Best
was sent to his rest as a Beatle, so Joe the poet
was axed from the famous volume that appeared
in Bristol, mostly because Cottle the publisher found
Joe's ballads too lachrymose and foolish:
The drowned kittens who haunted the murderer
until he hanged himself, and others even more ghoulish.
So Joe had to go, forever lost to fame and letters.

COUNTRY OF OLD MEN (FOR MY SEVENTIETH BIRTHDAY)

"that is no country for old men"

When you have to get up several times
during the night to empty your bladder
you know that you have arrived
in the country of old men.

When you number your past in a
cascade of decades as you contemplate
a future of possible single digits you know
that you really are in the country of the old.

When you turn to introduce
an old friend and draw a blank,
and when more of your friends
are dead than alive, then you begin
to appreciate that you've reached
a serious stage of advancing age.

When you can't remember things
you did long ago, then you can
rest assured you have an advanced
degree in growing and greying
beyond maturity.

When you observe the young
in each other's arms with
no trace of envy then you
know you're at a great remove
from who you once were.

When the thought of letting go
of all you know of this word
fails to fill you with dread and
you accept that all you've done
is so very little next to what
you might have achieved,
then you have to accept that
you are well beyond *forever young*
and that you've had your
passport stamped at the border
of the country of old men.

PAS DE *NOUVEAU* POUR MOI

"Plonger au fond du gouffre . . . pour trouver du *nouveau!*"

i

Bored Baudelaire, that Parisian *flaneur*
plagued by *ennui*
sought to plunge into the abyss
to find at its bottom
something *new.*

That is a risk I will gladly *not* take
nor do I think the French poet
really wanted to either: it
was only a rhetorical riff.
And to be bored in Paris
is in any case a poor
excuse for being alive.

Though I like heights now and then
for a good thrill, I will take
a pass for the time being on
taking a leap into the deep.

No abysses hold charms for me:
I prefer the old familiar places and faces.
I like the world I've come to know

in my six plus decades here below
with all its ups and downs,
its daily joys and horror shows
retailed on the evening news
between commercials.

I like the smell of strong coffee brewing in the morning,
I like a noontime nap, I like
listening to the wind in the trees,
and I like women who are a bit of a tease.

I like teaching Shakespeare when the class is awake,
and tennis doubles with the mantra
of "hold and break."

I like a glass of sherry or wine
before dinner, or an ice cold
beer on a hot summer day
to keep the doldrums at bay.

ii

At my stage of life I don't need
the *nouveau* to make me go.
I'm attached to the world I know.
The mirror reflection of the
branches mapped onto
the surface of the pond,
the blue heron feeding and then
taking wing make my heart sing.
A certain slant of light in the

fading of the crepuscular day
puts my mind at ease.

I don't thrill to the new.
It's the fear of having to let go
of all that's near and dear
that chills me to the bone.
In the balance sheet of
my ever-accumulating days
I see no entries for *ennui,*
nor any need to go in search
of the *nouveau.*

The knowledge of who and where
I am and all the things I've
been and done is quite
enough for me. I'm happy
to grant that my life is more
of a well-heeled cliché than
an aged wine's seasoned bouquet.

Whenever that final call to voyage
arrives I trust that I will be
ready to go and take the plunge
into that mysterious
fond du gouffre
when and if I must.

DEAD REYNARD

On a secluded path in the wood
he lay, the lithe young fox
with several neat puncture marks
on his neck, looking as if
he was asleep.

The kill was fresh,
but who did the killing?
Was it the coyotes we hear
howling in the night?
And why was he killed?
In a territorial fight, or for
the sheer thrill of it?

Was he surprised in an assault
from behind, or did he have
a chance to resist? The lack
of any signs of struggle suggests
a swift and sudden end.

Now a week later all that remains
is an array of lean bones picked
very clean. The small triangular
skull is positioned like an
exhibit for the passerby:

the russet reynard life reduced
to its skeletal core, so stark,
so elemental and so inanimate
there on the unfeeling ground.

NIGHT AND DAY

What you dream in the night
and what you live in the day

Are two different worlds
separated by a spider's thread
and a moonbeam.

What you live in the night
and what you dream in the day

Are two different worlds
separated by a spider's thread
and a moonbeam.

LATE SEPTEMBER

It's that time of year again:
the wide vista of trees with a spectrum of colors
ranging from green to yellow to crimson
against the blue wash of the sky.

On this cloudless day
the leaves drift to the ground
in the softest of all wind-
whispered landings.

The morning light comes later and crisper,
the reddish sun slips under the horizon
earlier and earlier.

The grass still grows but at a much
much slower pace. Only
a few solitary monarchs
veer by sporadically.

After it rains the small orange spotted
salamanders are few and
far between in the wood
where the green ferns still hold
out against the advancing
season as they fade to pale.

So far there's been only
the faintest trace of overnight
frost on the still-lush lawn.
At dawn the shrill silence
of late September
rings in our ears.

AT A BAROQUE CONCERT
[FOR GURDIP SETHI]

Nine musicians play in concert
a cavalcade of crystal clear
notes magisterially arrayed
like the golden band of
a miniature Milky Way.

Music is a remote but rarefied
echo of an infinitesimal segment
of the sonic syntax of the
unending sentence
that is the universe:

The distillation of the divine,
the invisible trace of the ground
of being, the distant and barely
audible intimation of what has been
and what will always be.

FLAWED PERFECTION

Even the most perfectly polished
mirror has a microscopic flaw at its center
not visible to the naked eye.

At the core of the glittering band
of the Milky Way there's a
black hole so massive even
gravity collapses in
upon itself.

An optimist sees only the mirror's polish
and the galaxy's glitter;
a pessimist only the crucial fault
that undoes the frame of each.

A realist sees both flaw and perfection,
but a sanguine idealist intuits
the pure Platonic archetype
behind the mirror
and on the other side
of the all-devouring vortex.

OLD MAN'S REINCARNATION FANTASY

Late in this lifetime I still
can't carry a tune or play
any instrument, but in my
next incarnation I will learn
to finger the blues guitar
like a virtuoso, Joe-Bonamassa-
or Eric-Clapton-like.

In this lifetime my little Latin
hardly gets me to Square One,
but in the next one I will apply
myself to Greek and Latin
as a schoolboy and master
them well enough to read
Homer and Horace in their
original tongues.

In this lifetime I've played tennis,
both singles and doubles,
for four decades plus, but
have never progressed beyond
advanced intermediate.

In the next life I will start hitting
the courts and whack the ball
as a boy, with indulgent parents

cheering me on, in order to
become the Roger Federer of
my generation by my mid-twenties.

Mere star dust that we are,
I don't see why the universe
shouldn't allow us the opportunity
of such multiple human incarnations.

FOR DANTE THOMAS (1922–2013)

You loved books both as material objects
and as companions of the mind.
You read and owned more of them
than anyone I know, and all
those books you loved to read
became a part of you. And
us: both bibliophile and mental
traveler, you gifted so many
by sharing what you loved.

A quiet magician and alchemist
of the inquiring mind, you traced
the mysteries of our being not
only in print, but also in the shapes
of the visible world in the black-
and-white photographs you
brought to life in the silent
vigils of your dark room.

In our noisy world of perpetual
self-trumpeting you kept true
in your own quiet way to
the touchstone of your best self.

In your final moments you looked
up with wide open eyes
of intense concentration.
Was this a parting vision
of that mysterious liminal place
that always and already was
the habitus of who you
truly were?

Dear Dante, I trust that what
was once a seeking pilgrim soul
in death is now made whole.

NOVEMBER CREPUSCULE

Between the skeletal trees stripped almost
entirely of leaves the disk of the
nearly full moon looms large.
A solitary moth flutters by.

In the far distance loud shotguns blasts
signal the opening of the deer
hunting season. These don't disturb
my dog crunching through the crisp
layers of dry leaves, chasing
some invisible scent buried in
late autumn's near-monochrome quilt.

Now he squats on his haunches
and gazes at me as I stare mesmerized
at the gibbous moon in the fading light
of this mid-November late afternoon.

ON THE OUTSIDE LOOKING IN

To the one on the outside looking in
the warm glow of the room is as far
away and as alien as empty space.
The thin glass that shuts him out is
an arctic ocean of denial and despair.

To the one sealed in the exile
of his abandoned hopes
the sidewalk is a concrete
universe inhabited by no one
but himself as he gazes into
what is forever far
beyond his reach.

Inside he sees
lips moving, hands
gesticulating, but he
hears not a word.

To the one outside looking in
there is no other way
to be
but the utter silence
of his singularity.

THAT GRIM REAPER

You google an old college friend
you lost touch with after you both
graduated back in 1966.
He played the dobro guitar
and introduced you to Bluegrass,
including your first and favorite
Bluegrass song, "Come all ye fair
and tender ladies."
So you google his name,
and this is what you find:
"R. W. E. died on June 14, 2010,
after a six-month battle with cancer."
He was sixty-six.

And you are seventy and stunned.
But still alive and kicking.
Yes. Alive still. Yes.

You call a mutual college friend
to give him the bad news
and share memories.
He tells you that his first wife,
a college classmate and friend,
died last year.
An acute alcoholic.

Two days later you carelessly scan
the obituary pages of the *New York Times*
Sunday edition and you casually
glimpse the name of another
college classmate who passed away
after receiving a stem cell transplant.

That goddamned Grim Reaper is
a relentless serial killer
thinning the ranks
of your old friends.

Tough as nails, hard as bricks,
Pennsylvania '66
was our proud class slogan.
Nails and bricks fade like grass
in the passing wind
that blows us from ourselves
God only knows where.
Goddamn that Grim Reaper.

I listen to the Bluegrass station
hoping for it to play *Come all*
ye fair and tender ladies,
take a warning how
ye court your men,
they're like the stars on
a summer morning,
they first appear,
and then they're gone.

Tempus fugit,
going, going, gone.
Dust in the wind,
that's all we are,
dust in the wind,
yes we are.
Ou sont les neiges d'antan?
Going, going, gone.

DECEMBER 20, 2013

A green omelet, the frozen pond
lies surrounded by an expanse
of white snow and a distant
tree line outlined against the
somber fog-draped hills.

The moist air hangs upon the silence
of this ultimate autumn afternoon.
Tomorrow winter will come in
with relays of rain.

Christmas will be washed out:
sodden fields for my
Weimaraner and I
to slosh through,
our feet finding the way.

Like the bobcats we never see
the New Year remains in hiding,
biding its time,
waiting to pounce.

TRACKS IN THE SNOW

A thick layer of freshly fallen snow
covers my old tracks in the wood.
I try to retrace the familiar steps,
but keep on missing my way.
I seek to go where I've gone before,
but only end up missing the mark
and going astray.

So it is with our past when
we try to recover who
and what we once were.
Our best efforts only confound
themselves as we strive to
backtrack to the old trails
we once walked with ease.
To try to revisit the paths we
took decades ago is only
to err in a blurred world.

Even as I trek in search of
where I once walked
the falling flakes quickly cover
the prints I leave in my wake.

CHRISTMAS EVE, ZELL AM SEE, 1950

The midnight mass we went to
after the lighting of the wax
candles on the fragrant tree and the
magical sparklers and the singing
of *stille Nacht, heilige Nacht*
and the opening of my present
there under the dark green fir branches

I do not remember.

But the going to the Mass and the
coming home from the Mass
in my brand-new brown felt-lined
rubber boots through the fresh snow
and how they shone in the night
like the ice crystals drifting
in the frozen air and the
unspeakable delight of my first walk
in those wonderful Christmas boots

that I do remember.

CADILLACS

On my first visit to Atlantic City
on a day trip when I was not quite
fifteen in the summer of 1958
I wandered into a Cadillac showroom.
I had my hands all over the shiny
cars, fingering the tailfins flaring
out wing-like past the trunk and
the glossy chrome bumpers.

With my hands on the large steering
wheel, I eyed the vast dashboard
gleaming with mysterious dials,
the regal shift lever, the lush
leather upholstery, pretending
I was driving the car down
the avenue, wide-eyed tourists
in envious awe, lesser cars
like Chevys and Fords and
Plymouths paying tribute,
mere legionnaires in my royal
and triumphal procession.

THE PURSUIT OF GLORY

"Chief occupation . . . pursuit of glory"
(Robert Frost, according to "Who's Who")

The pursuit of glory is no easy task.
What you get falls far short of what you ask.
You keep plodding on as you grow old
finding what you've pursued may be fool's gold.
The reward you so eagerly sought when young
now doesn't even seem worth the song.
But like the panther pacing in his cage
day after day you've built up a great reserve
of patience waiting for what you deserve.
You wonder if that day will ever come
or if in your seventies it has already gone.
You stiffen your spine for the lean years ahead
knowing that all who aspire end up dead.
You're not quite old enough for the resignation of age
but too far along to indulge in mere fits of rage.

EARLY JANUARY

Already January has shown its
two faces, visiting a weather see-saw
upon us: heavy snows that soon
melt, followed by a full-blown
arctic blast bottoming out at
minus four Fahrenheit not
counting the wind-chill factor.

Gingerly we walk the woods
on polished ice. And then comes
the sudden warm-up peaking
at fifty degrees with torrential
downpours. The soggy ground
sucks at our boots as we
pace the familiar paths under
the melting ice and snow.

The pond, full to the brim,
reflects a ghostly geometry of
tree trunks and interlacing branches.
We talk as we walk, our voices
lost in the bewildered landscape.

NIGHT VIGIL

Out here in the near wilderness
where we live the silence at night
is sometimes almost absolute.

Occasionally the whoosh and whine
of a distant jetliner interrupts
the deep quiet. For hours on
end everything seems stilled
to its very core. But then
in the last spell of the dark
before the first rays of dawn
a high-pitched whine or howl
invades the silence in a most
mysterious way. What is it
that I hear so eerily?

The coyotes calling on the cusp
of the coming of dawn?
The foxes' mating calls?
Or could it be the rumored
mountain lions whose sightings
have been reported at
secondhand but that
never are confirmed?

ARRESTED

Arrested in my walk—
the material world out there,
the irrefrangible reality
so simply given—I
cannot begin to fathom.

And what is, is yet so
very mysterious.
In that very fathomlessness
I make my stand,
I pause and take in
what cannot be taken in,

all the opaque that is there
beyond my grasp that
we take for granted,
the material world
inside and outside of us
everywhere.

Arrested I stand.

Where the Light Falls

EGYPTIAN NOTES

"Who are these coming to the sacrifice?"

They were an itinerant Egyptian quartet
on a Greek tour arranging
gigs as best they could.

In Thessaly an impromptu opportunity
arose at a wedding party
featuring a blood sacrifice.

As they readied their instruments
they watched the fine blade
slice through the heifer's silken flesh.

Mesmerized by the flow of blood
they thought of Isis and Osiris
separated and dispersed among the stars

And of the dark god of the sun Ra
and the warm waters of the Blue Nile
and how odd their Oriental instruments—

Flute, harp, lyre, and sistrum—
would sound to the young lovers
lost in their elongated kiss.

HAMLET SOUS RATURE

My lord, I did intend it.
    A damned defeat was made.
My pulse as yours does doth temperately keep time.
    I mean, my head upon your lap?
What speech, my good lord?
    Marry, well said, very well said.
If it assume my noble father's person.
    Made men and not made them well.
What wilt thou do? Thou wilt not murder me?
    She is so conjunctive to my life and soul.
When that her golden couplets are disclosed.
    Cries cuckold to my father, brands the harlot.
So you mis-take your husbands.
    My lord, as I was sewing in my closet.

TURNING

You turn
and I turn
and we turn

We turn because
in this world nothing
ever stays in place.

We turn in a turning world.
I turn because I cannot
not turn. I turn not
knowing that I turn.

When I choose to turn
I know that I cannot
make a wrong turn
only to discover
that I turn out of turn.

You, I, and we turn
in a turning world
knowing that we cannot
help but turn.

Our turning others us.
Others turn us.

We turn into others,
others into us.

We turn to find ourselves
for the first time
where we were
before we ever started
turning
only to find ourselves
turning to return.

RUMINANT

Unresolved he sits
in his unsettled seventies
looking out at the late autumn
hills and the leafless trees'
skeletal reflections in the pond.

For decades he assumed
that at some point some
higher knowledge would seep
into his recalcitrant brain.

Now he only takes in those around him
like a stranger passing through.
Most of the time he simply observes
without focus or desire
waiting for he knows not what.

He's acquired patience
like a stone its mossy crown.
His steady heartbeat
is a pedestrian metronome
measuring his humdrum days.
Not having found his function
all that he can affirm
is his ongoing impasse.

He ruminates without result,
he chews the cud of a
residual memory wiped
clean of all affect.

His passing moments
mark no real time
and are of no moment.

FIFTEEN SALAMANDERS

On our morning walk
in the damp wood
after the night rain
we counted fifteen salamanders:

Bright orange tongues of flame
on the moist ground,
such small and frail
shoots of new life

Innocent as Eve on her first
day in Paradise,
ancient as the history
of the world miniaturized.

NO PARABLE

On his final journey to Jerusalem
the Son of Man
stopped at a leafy fig tree
because he was hungry.

But to his grief all he found
was leaves and not a single fig.
So he cursed it to nevermore bear fruit.

The next day the disciples saw
that unlucky tree withered
down to its very roots.

This is no parable, but simply
goes to show that even Jesus
could sometimes throw a hissy fit.

WALKING

I've walked in the pine- and fir-scented air
through heather and bracken and up rock-strewn
moraines. I've had no hesitation to dare
trek for hours in bleak landscapes hewn
and glacier sculpted thousands of years ago.
I've braved the sun and wind and rain and snow
mulling thoughts as my feet paced the earth below.
Whatever I can glimpse in my questing mind
on my footloose journeys in this strange world
is a hidden treasure only I can find
in this stream of being into which we are hurled.
I've walked these paths knowing I'm not blind
because these thoughts that come as they will
keep me moving even when my feet are still.

INGOLSTADT

A lifetime ago on a road trip through Southern Germany
I spent a night in a Gasthaus in Ingolstadt, near
Munich. Until then I had simply assumed that the town
was only a figment of Mary Shelley's moonlit fantasies.

After dinner I ventured out for a long walk, crossed a stone
bridge over a current-rippling stream, sensing how odd it was
to be in this fabled place, thinking of young Victor
bent over the body remnants he was assembling, wondering
which house held his secret laboratory on its attic floor
as he worked frenetically through the long nights
to sculpt his Creature's uncouth form and jolt it
into life. Uneasily I sensed the presence of the student
of unhallowed arts, and sensed too his hapless creation,
born only to be orphaned, adrift and unanchored,
hiding somewhere in a nearby wood or copse, that lost,
bewildered and abandoned soul blundering through
a hostile world, seeking his absconded maker,
seeking some link to connect him with the human family.

Surely there should be a plaque in the town square
to commemorate the midnight shadows
that visited a nineteen-year-old girl's waking dream
whose phantasmagoric and hieratic forms
have been with us for some two centuries, ciphering
who and what we are at our best and our worst,

casting a long arc into futurity. So I thought
as I paced the spectral streets of Ingolstadt
in search of palpable presences unseen.
Their distant traces peopled my troubled mind
and I could almost grasp them there in that
alien German town's haunted air.

STAIN

The Stain that is History spreads and
soaks into us. Like blotting paper
we take it in. Whether we know it
or not, it permeates us. It seeps
into our marrow, our blood, our
cells, our nerves and very neurons.
It's both inside and outside of us.

We are the acted upon as much
as we are the actors and agents.
The Stain spreads far beyond us
like ripples on the surface of a pond
that never cease. As we blot it up
it blots us out. We are replete
with it, bloated like corpses after
drowning. It infects us, like a disease
that we pass on, Aids or Ebola-like.
We can deny but not escape it.
It haunts us into our graves
and is the midwife to the next
keening generation incubating
and waiting to be born.

HERBARIUM

Rousseau's *herbier* housing a
a gathering of dried plants was
his memory bank of landscapes
he had explored on his walks.
I have only to open my herbier and
soon it will transport me there
he wrote in his lyrical *Reveries*,
luxuriating in his later years
in that mnemonic transport.

My version of Rousseau's herbarium
is an old US Army footlocker in my
basement that I was given as a boy.
I haven't opened it in many a year.

Perhaps I fear it's a Pandora's box,
and the scraps of my distant past it
contains may curse and haunt me
in the here and now like the imaginary
demons under the bed of a crying
child's torturing night fears.

But more likely it only holds shards
of a superannuated and long
forgotten past, the bits and pieces
of my early years, sentimental

flotsam of who I once was and now
can barely bother to recall:

A junior high yearbook, old
pocket calendars with scribbled notes
whose meaning now escapes me,
a cheap watch whose ticking regulated
my childish days, a much-fingered deck
of cards that my small hands thrilled to
hold, my first communion candle redolent
of the odor of warm wax and wafting incense,
and more such mementos charged with
associations that once moved my heart
but that are now mere detritus signifying
a rapidly receding and dwindling past.

HERMIONE'S RESURRECTION

"Music, awake her, strike!"

For sixteen years I dwelt sequestered,
my cloistered flesh frozen almost
to stone in what seemed the very
stasis of time. My issue was
unknown, lost with Antigonus in
the wilds of an alien world.

My deranged spouse now come to
his senses made his daily
visit to my grave, sorrowful
and penitence-stricken under
Paulina's watchful gaze.
She kept my secret, and I
kept my own sad counsel
in the hiatus of my protracted
thoughts, the very flow of
my blood almost suspended.

Perdita suddenly found
broke that protracted spell.
Boldly posed in marble,
with furrowed face I held
my very breath as Paulina
exhibited me to Leontes
and our blooming daughter,

both enraptured by such a
lifelike work of art. Their faith
awakened by the magic of music,
they beheld the wonder of my
descent from the pedestal as
marble turned to flesh once more
when I took them by the hand,
my family made whole the
instant I re-entered the joy
and terror of temporality.

TO MY MUSE

During my hapless adolescence
I wooed you in intermittent fits
convinced that the poetic excrescences

I poured forth were manna scattered from Olympian
skies. The poor imitations I wrought in my
decades-long dedication to you

Left a prolific trail of paper, the long
legend of my labored efforts
as I sought in vain the necessary boon

Of my own voice intoning the eternal
melodies that haunted my dreams
and that half-awake I heard in the wind,

In the trees, in the water in the stream,
in the cloud-swept skies, in the flight
of birds, in the dim glimmer of the remotest

Stars. In a blind world I heard them
and sought to make them heard
but year after year I found only deaf ears.

Undeterred I persisted through the lean decades.
A grizzled veteran of the long haul
I have ceased to calculate the loss or gain.

With my eyes firmly fixed on the receding
horizon I can only affirm that in my calloused
faith I have been true to you in my fashion.

SONNET 130 RE-PETRARCHIANIZED

My mistress's eyes by far outshine the sun;
Her lips are redder than the reddest coral's red;
Next to her breasts the whitest snow is dun;
Shiny as black silk is the glossy hair on her head.
I have seen roses damasked, red and white,
But the splendor of her cheeks far surpasses these,
And if in some perfumes I have found delight
Next to her sweet breath they smell like foul cheese.
When I hear her super melodious voice I know
That no music can ever match her pleasing sound.
I grant I never saw a goddess go
But know my mistress's feet deify the ground.
I have no doubt that my love is so rare
Any she could only match her by false compare.

GRUDGES

At the funeral service of a friend
her daughter recalled her telling her
she should never hold a grudge because
it would slowly eat away at her.

This hit home to me: the sun
shining through a stained
glass window suddenly lit up
my soul and in my mind's eye
I saw a host of coruscated
dark spots, a sinful honeycomb
of long ingrained resentments,
the bitter sum of all the grudges
big and little I've ever held
in my long life, the poison fruit
I have so assiduously cultivated.

Such a soul I thought surely
could never leave this earth,
having become earth,
having taken on its dark taint.
Too often and too long I've
lived my life as if it were
a mere grudge match, seeking
to get even, as if tit for tat
was a moral balance sheet

and not the way to ruin
my best self in the corrosive
acid bath of futile anger.

There in the church pew I thought
that even late in the game we can
open our hearts to let the world in
and rise above the frozen waste
of mere resentment. If aging
souls are like tarnished silver,
there may still be time to restore
their original shine.

PHOTOGRAPH OF PRISONERS AT BUCHENWALD CONCENTRATION CAMP, APRIL 1945

In black and white seventeen of them stand
behind barbed wire on the day of their liberation.
Emaciated figures in circus-striped pantaloons
and jackets, grotesque survivors who have cheated
death. The vertical bars of their camp uniforms
and the rectangles of the wired wall
make for an odd geometry sundering
the viewer from the viewed. Three of
the men in the front row have a hand
calmly resting on the wire. The grim
group stares intently at the photographer.

Are we viewing them, or are they viewing us
across an unbridgeable gulf? The piercing eyes
in their emaciated faces look directly at us but also
right through us into a far distance we cannot
begin to fathom. The Mephistopheles of
the poet who lived at the Court of the
Muses in Weimar more than two centuries ago
is child's play next to this infernal alien
scene beyond the pale of what we still cannot
quite process some seven decades later.
The picture shows this is no place for Muses.

Behind barbed wire these men on the verge
of their departure are like birds in a cage.
One handsome youth's pale face radiates
a riveting blend of passionate grief and
fierce anger. To his left another has
his right hand in his pocket and his left arm
crooked, with fingers at his chin and lips.
Abstracted in quizzical contemplation,
he is the Horatio of Buchenwald.
To his left a twenty-something with
protruding ears seems quietly resigned
to his unknown fate. A man in his fifties
is propped on a cane whose diagonal slant
unsettles the symmetry of the scene.
His limp eyes convey a plaintive despair
beyond anger or reproach. On the far
left stands a tall man in his late thirties
whose piled black cap and gaunt intellectual's
face make him look like an academic
on the dais of a graduation ceremony.
His erect posture and defiantly impervious
eyes attest the undefeated spirit of
a soul who has seen it all.

These striped men have harrowed
the hell that is the human heart
at its worst and have survived
to gaze at us with a knowledge
latent deep in our bones that we never
want to acknowledge or confront as
the perennial burden of our being
who and what we are.

Their release will disperse them in
space and time, but bring no
resolution to the terrible riddle
of their being there nor its repetition
in different incarnations and variable
scales of magnitude in the eternal return
of the years and centuries to come.

RECHERCHE

The *recherche du temps perdu* is a futile quest.
The past is a country you can't visit
because your passport expired long ago.

The past you think you recall
is only as a construct in your mind,
a story that changes with every telling.
There's no hard drive from which
its corrupted file can be recovered.

The past is an imaginary refuge
for escapees who can't escape
the burdens of today that
tomorrow too will be shredded
remainders of someone else's dreams.

EQUINOX

There's a kind of equinox in
our later years, a turning or
a tipping point:

When we've lived long enough
sooner or later
we will find

A phenomenon most unkind:
more people that we know
are dead than alive.

True, we survive
but the roots in the soil of
our sociability are sundered.

So we live on more solitary
by the day, Tithonus-like
as more and more of

Our past slips away.
The undiscovered country
still awaits us.

So many we have known
have gone before us
in the perennial harvest
of the Great Unknown.

The landscape of our lives
is depopulating
even as we seek to stand
our ground and stay in place.

Death is the unrelenting wind
that perpetually strips the leaves
from life's autumnal trees.

BEAUTIFUL PEOPLE

Here's a truism tried and true:
even the Beautiful People have to die too.
No matter how brightly their glamor shone
they have to go into the Great Void alone.
It may not be much of a consolation
that they too have to face it with trepidation
even as their fleeting fame's glittering career
was lived mostly on the surface of life's veneer.

THE DAILY NEWS

Nature does what nature can
to unsettle the estate of man
with earthquake, fire, and flood,
but it's what man does to man in cold blood
that is enough to make even the Devil
amazed at the ingenious extent of our evil.

INVISIBLE SCARS

We can't see the hidden scars
that even the most bright-faced
carry as stigmata on their souls.
We don't notice how they sweat
under the accumulated griefs
that they carry like backpacks
whose weight only they can feel.

This secret freight we all bear
though to the uncaring world
it may seem as light as a feather
and as transparent as the air.
But secretly it's always there.

Even in the best weather
the happiest and most carefree
among us are thus inevitably
worn and borne down,
fraught with our hidden griefs,
our covert woes that gather
and descend upon us like a cloud.

They are nothing else but the sheer
burden of our being human
which at best we can endure
and sometimes even embrace as
the deep-dyed signature of our lives.

In the end it's our very scars
that make us who and what we are.

ROOTS

We see the tree,
the branches, the leaves,
the blossoms, and the fruit

But we do not see
the roots that reach far down into the earth
with fingers of infinity.

EYES WIDE OPEN

"I will encounter darkness as a bride / And hug it in mine arms" [Shakespeare]

"that immortal sea / Which brought us hither" [Wordsworth]

1

Eyes wide open,
fully awake,
that is how I want
to go out:
wide awake
to see if there's
anything to see:
perhaps periodic flares
as the mind goes dark.

How can that which has come into being
go out of being and be nothing?
Can the dying hug the darkness
as a bride? Or is that only
a necrophiliac fantasy?

2

Is death a double dealer
who will take us by surprise?
Could it be the start
of something entirely new?
Or is that merely
wishful thinking?

The fact is that nobody
from the greatest sage
to the lowliest drudge
really has a clue.

Or if there are clues
we don't see them,
or if we see them,
we don't know how to read them.
Death is the undeciphered
Rosetta Stone.

3

Eyes wide open, yet we're blind.
Eyes wide open is what I aspire to,
eyes wide open,
yet nobody knows.

A plunge into the Deep
of that Primordial Sea
not knowing if or when
you will ever surface again.
With eyes wide open
even then I want to go.

4

We all come in
without a choice,
we all go out
without a choice.
From the primordial ocean
we come,
to the primordial ocean
we go.

THE TOUR BUS FROM DACHAU

The simple block letters DACHAU
were prominently displayed
on the windshield of the German
tour bus parked in the main square
of my Austrian hometown
in the mid-1950s. I was just
a boy then, but still those letters
had a sinister ring that the quaint
murmur of the fountain in the square
could not quite muffle. The dark
taint of the concentration camp cast
a pall over our small tourist town.

The parked bus was empty;
its occupants must have been
out walking down by the flower-
bedded lake promenades,
or sitting in a café. In the
green ignorance of my youth
I could not help but wonder
what these tourists from Dachau
had been up to during the war,
and why they were so crass
as to go on vacation sporting
that notorious death's head name
in a coach that for all I know

might have been an express
come straight from Hell.

SINGLE LEAF

The mid-November ground
is thickly blanketed
with dry leaves whose
colors have mostly faded
to a listless brown.
In the bare-branched trees
only a few ghostly leaves
hang on against the odds.
On this windless day
occasionally a single one
slowly drifts to the ground
between the skeletal trees.

WHERE THE LIGHT FALLS

Where the light falls
at the dying of the day
before it fades away
is where I take my stand.

No postures or poses,
no need for before
or after when I'm in

that place. The frost-
whited lawn at dawn
the rising harvest moon
can have their way

but I stay where the light
falls. I simply take it in
as the gift it always is:

The perpetual present
of my passing life
at the dying of the day
where I take my stand.

EAGLES OF DEATH [PARIS, FRIDAY, NOVEMBER 13, 2015]

The Eagles of Death were playing
on the stage when the real
eagles of death entered
the theater and vented
their cold-blooded rage
in the indiscriminate stutter
of AK-47 gunfire and exploding
hand grenades. As the band
fled some dazed and blood-
spattered survivors were
able to stagger out of
the corpse-littered theater
into the siren-screaming
chaos of the streets.

The eagles of death have landed
again and their horrific deeds
still echo in our stunned minds.
The corpses in the shaken
metropolis haunt our dreams as
horrific harbingers of a fate
omnipresent in our instantly
connected and terror-ridden world.

WHAT IS

What is, is said pre-Socratic Parmenides.
I pick up different books and read some pages
to gather fragments of wisdom from the sages
hoping to gather from all these
more than mere tautologies.

Too often I find only empty words
and abstractions that drive me to distraction.
The beingness of being is in its being
is the kind of ontological spoof
I'm sick and tired of seeing.

If according to Parmenides being is only one
then you and I are essentially none.
The immense multiplicity of the world
can't be put into words.
Being is entirely beyond what anyone can say
though nevertheless we live it every day.

LANDING A POEM

I would like to land a poem
the way a boxer lands a blow.
I want that poem to be just so.

I want it to stay in the memory
like a great wave on an endless sea.
I want it to sing like a song
that you can't unhear,
a melody so clear
you carry it with you
wherever you go
your whole life long.

I want that poem to become
the gist of what is most true of you,
a voice from your astral plane
that calls you home again.

GEDANKENSPIEL

In a deep-tranced silence they sit
rapt in contemplation,
fingering pellucid glass beads,
moving them along lines visible
only in their minds.

These translucent beads
are the hard currency
of long-protracted thought
earned in pure concentration
seeking to embrace the universe.

Its infinite variety is expressed
in these miniature crystalline marbles
moved swiftly by hand in a sublime charade,
an improvised yet infinitely reflective
game at whose base are math and music.

Gedankenspiel of *The Glass Bead Game*:
the perennial play of the mind
at once so sterile and yet so serene.

GRIM RECOGNITION

That striped fellow liked to sun himself
on a flagstone by our front door
and groom his face with his tiny paws.
Behind the glass-paneled door
our dog would bark furiously
to no effect whatever.

But one golden autumn day the chipmunk
thought he was playing a game
of hide-and-seek with the dog,
darting in and out among the
trees and bushes, veering
at sharp angles, skittering
with manic energy

until the moment when
he was firmly seized between strong
teeth that scored deep gashes in
the striped fellow's sides,

and the smirk on his face
was replaced at the wide-
eyed instant of death
with the rictus of recognition

that this had been no game.

RACQUETBALL MEMORIAL

Alone on the court I'm
practicing my game
surrounded by shadows:

There's grinning Don who makes
a winning shot that caroms off
the side wall to barely touch
the lowest part of the front panel,
Don who many years ago
cracked his head against the back wall
and nearly died of a hematoma
before he really died of
a rare pulmonary disease.

There's Bill who stopped playing
long before he left us for good
whose bearded jerky moves
on the court were hard to fathom
and who succumbed to
some sort of dementia.

There's Joe who indulged in Pepsi
and chips so long that
he started to look like
the Michelin Man but who
in his heyday had some

cunning shots to die for
before pancreatitis
did him in.

And then there's Randy
who despite his football-
scarred knees could move
with the stealth of a panther
as he expertly put the ball
just out of my reach, whose
ear had been bloodied from
being smacked by a racquet
and who fought his melanoma
with his last dying breath.

I'm on the court spellbound
amidst moving shadows that
silently hit balls off the ceiling
and into the front corners,
a ghostly dance of revenants
who haunt my mind as after
images of lives once lived
and still alive in me.

FARM DELIVERY TO YOUNG SAMUEL TAYLOR COLERIDGE

On a breezy summer day in 1798
the man on business from Porlock came
to the door of the solitary farmhouse
near Linton because he had a delivery
for someone known by the initials S. T. C.

After he repeatedly knocked on the oak
door, a dreamy-eyed, long-haired young
fellow emerged from the parlor room
to accept what the man had brought:
a case of bottles filled with laudanum.
S. T. C. stood and stared distraught
as if he couldn't grab ahold of a single
thought. He looked like he'd been
fast asleep, lost deep in a trance,
but he held a pen in his hand
which he used to sign the receipt.

The man from Porlock put the case
down as the poet with flashing eyes
and floating hair uttered some phrases
about Xanadu and pleasure domes
and caves of ice and thick pants
and a sacred river and demon lovers
and a damsel with a dulcimer and
melons and honeydew from paradise.

The delivery man was so surprised
he couldn't believe his ears
or eyes. So he shook his head
and headed straight back
to town, looking around now
and then as if he'd seen a ghost.

LIGHT A LAMP

The lotus-smiling golden Buddha
in the calendar on the wall of my study
is headed by the quote, "If you light a lamp
for someone else, it will also brighten
your own path." That I like: If only
I could light someone's path
or even lighten their burden.

It would be a pleasure to know that I've
helped to show someone else the way.
To light a lamp for someone you have to
be able to think beyond yourself, which
isn't easy to do when you can't even
see what's in front of you. It's so nice
of these smiling sages to deliver such
edifying and uplifting sentiments, but
I can't help but wonder if that golden
grin of enlightenment isn't an ignus fatuus
blinding them to the inevitable darkness
that is our common human heritage.

CELL PHONES STILL RING (ORLANDO, JUNE 13, 2016)

Among the sprawl of bloodied bodies
cell phones still ring, their sounds
a dark cloud, a shroud for a night
of sheer terror, a bloodbath we have
seen and dread to see again. The phones
still ring for no one to answer; at the
other end are those who in the suspense
of silence hope in vain to hear a voice
against diminishing odds. These sounds
are prayers in the void, a bleak and
sinister dirge for those poor souls
who had no intimation that in a single
horrific instant their joyful dancing
would be transformed into a dance of death.

HONG KONG (JUNE 2016)

City vertical, buildings rising far up
into the sky, floor after floor,
city of malls and banks and corporate
headquarters, city of crowded
sidewalks and packed subway
cars with half the people glued
to their smartphones, city
of sun-filtered mist and clouds,
city ringed by rugged mountains
with sheer cliffs, city of gated
mansions on high, city of cars
and buses speeding in huge
numbers, city of perpetual swarms
of people on the move, bustling
metropolis, so civilized, so regulated,
so chaotic, so much on the make,
so old and yet so new, city of
the new century teeming and
gleaming with skyscrapers.

DEEP-ROOTED (COLLEGE GARDEN, NEW COLLEGE, OXFORD, AUGUST 2016)

With hands spread wide I greet
again an ancient massive friend,
a centuries-old deep-rooted
tree. I press against its rough
bark to feel a hint of vital
bioenergy transfer itself to me,

to sense the flow of its life force
rise from the deep earth
where its gnarled tentacle roots
are anchored, to touch a residue
of the eons to suffuse
my inner being, to gain

some of the primeval endurance
of that huge-limbed primordial trunk,
to help ground and anchor me
in the soil of our humanity,
to provide a deep-rooted foundation
for my uncertain and unknown future.

MID-AUGUST AGAIN (CONESUS, NEW YORK, AUGUST 17, 2016)

"Season of mists and mellow fruitfulness"

The mid-August light filters through
a thick-branched screen of lush green
leaves. There's no hint yet of the
mellow season, save for that in the
moss-damp and fern-decked wood
now and then a single yellow leaf drifts
prematurely to the silent ground.

To be anchored back home,
feet planted firmly as the round
of the seasons proceeds in a
forever turning and chaotic world,
is my humble wish and hope. And
wishing is maybe all we mere mortals
can aspire to in our uncertain lives.

Keats lived to see another autumn
in his posthumous life in Rome,
and even in the slow agony of his
so early death he made perhaps
the most graceful epistolary bow
that any poet has ever made.

And here I am in the green hills above
Hemlock Lake a day short of seventy,
nearly three times his age. I will
make my way through the seasons
in the hills and woods above the lake
through snow and rain and wind and sun,
sifting my random fleeting thoughts
to see if there are any nuggets to be found
in the sediment of my mental sieve.

I know that autumn and the soft-dying days
will be here soon enough, and then the
leaden and bitter-cold skies of winter,
but I also know that spring will inevitably
come around again. I hope to feel its rising
sap in my aging bones. I'm far from ready
yet to take my final bow.

Some Things

THINGS

I'm looking for something
but I don't know what it is
or where to find it.

A missing key, perhaps,
or a long-lost watch,
or something that's
almost on the tip of my tongue.

Perhaps it's in a Lost
and Found somewhere
that I can't ever find. Or
maybe it's always just
beyond the line of my
ever-receding horizon.

DINGLICHKEIT

It's the irrefrangible *thingness*
of the world that sticks in the craw
of the mind as the ineluctable
condition of our being.
Like it or not, our senses'
ground or grounding they
are. We can reduce or abstract
them to a string of words,
but our world is flooded with
them to the point of repletion
through mass production and
exchange across continents and cultures.

Things are the junk food of
the soul, the daily fix we crave yet
feel constricted and afflicted by.
Without them what would or could
we be, surrounded, served, controlled
by them, comforted, frustrated,
what are we more than things
among things?

Our essential
and inescapable *thingness*
at once unhinges and enables
our thinking as the currency

without which we could never
negotiate the markets of our
irremediably material world.

COLORADO COLLEGE SCENE
(OCTOBER 2016)

A manicured lawn stretches to
a mesh wire fence. Students skim by
on bicycles on the other side where
in the far distance there are
walkers and joggers. An unseen
voice is issuing directions to
athletes on a practice field.

The late afternoon sun gilds luminous
autumn foliage. In the far distance
there's the steady metronome of
truck tires and the occasional
grinding of freight train wheels.
The rugged high Rocky Mountains
are framed by a crystalline blue sky.

A frisbee arcs through the air as two
young men, bare to the waist, catch
and throw with practiced precision.
Students pass by in twos and threes.
High up several white jet plumes
cut tangents across the blue expanse.

On this warm and dry afternoon
the crisp air of early evening begins
to approach on cats' paws. The sun

still warms the walls of orange buildings that will radiate the heat long after it has set. In the perpetual whirl and flux of passing moments, the very *thingness* of the world.

DING AN SICH

The Thing-in-Itself isn't really
a thing but an idea of something
we're not capable of thinking
on the other side of a limit
we can't pass. Things we can
think, but not the Thing-In-Itself:
Res cogitans, or the perpetual
traffic between ideas and things.

LATE NOVEMBER

The whooshing sound of leaves
layered on the ground as feet
traverse them is both material and
spiritual. The gathering detritus
of a fading season, leaves
are also the language of the
soul. They wing their way
to the ground only to turn
in time into a mere monochrome.

The fecund earth is fertilized
by millennia of such seasons
of fallen leaves. A white
shroud of first snow is in
the offing. Those few belated
leaves still descending and
all that heaped leaf refuse:

the departing year shedding its skin.

IDEAS

The material world in its near
infinite variety of forms
is available to the senses.
Its multitude of thinged profusion
is sorted into patterns,
rearranged and constructed by them.

Ideas are not thus available.
Unlike things, they are not
contained in or by space
and time. Uncontained,
unconstrained, undefined
by mere matter. All things
come and go, be it in
a millisecond or a billion
years, but immaterial
ideas know no now,
no before or after, but
simply are: have always
been, will always be.

THINGS UNTHINKABLE

When suddenly the unexpected and unthinkable
occurs, things appear in an entirely different
light. What was once invisible can now be seen,
what was once taboo can now be spoken
and heard by all, what was once utterly
beyond the pale is now the new *du jour*.

The shape of things has completely
changed at one fell swoop. The hidden
is here and now, said out loud without
any pretense of reserve. Soon the new
order of the day will be so routine that
once again it will be unheard and unseen.
The familiar world is still there in vestigial form
but nothing will ever be the same again.

ACROBATS

High up in the circus tent
the acrobats pirouette in the air,
soar and glide like birds where
hidden ropes hold or catch

Them in their sleek flight
to meet pairs of hands
as wide-eyed children stare in fright
to see if and where they land.

With practiced ease and rhythmic pace
they risk their lives every day
in an ethereal dance of such grace
it takes our very breath away.

We're filled with such delight
to behold their unearthly skill
that for days on end we still
recall the acrobats' aerial flight.

CLEOPATRA

The serpent of the Nile who beguiled
the Roman general, the Egyptian impresario
of passion's wayward ways, had the asp
brought to her in a leaf-wreathed basket
of figs. Rather than bow to the young
conqueror who had undone Antony
at Actium, she clasped it between her sleek
breasts to let the poison bred in the fertile
river's mud bite into her dun flesh,
savoring the bitter joy of that deadly worm.

The actress of consummate caprice
who had played her erotic charades
with the makers and the shakers
of that ancient world scripted
her final act as a *pièce de résistance*
to rise above them all and show
that she could go the distance.

Fire and air her rarefied legacy,
her dying dream to rejoin Marc Antony
unwithered, unstaled by custom,
fresh as the very first dawn,
ancient as the final sunset
of a forever-dying world.

CHEMIN DES POIRIERS
[FOR BETSY CATHRO]

In my memory of Pear Lane
in Champagne sur Seine things
are always pretty much the same
in that big house in which
we lived with the stone balustrade
leading down to the front lawn.

This was in the 1950s.
In the long summers
my niece Betsy and I rode
our bicycles up and down
the Chemin. I was twelve
and she was seven then.
But all that ended when her
father suddenly died. We
grieved and went our separate
ways as our numbed lives
diverged. They never really
merged again.

Two weeks ago the news
of her death at sixty-nine
sucker punched me in the gut
and took away my very breath.
But in the mirrored museum
of my elongating past Pear Lane

will always remain very
much the same.

In memory's bittersweet remit
the trees whose pears we
never got around to picking
are still there, budding
every spring in that provincial
French town's pastoral air.

ALL ALONE

You walk into a room where your
octogenarian father is sitting
by himself. He is quietly sobbing,
his face a contorted mask of
sheer grief. You ask him what's
wrong, but he refuses to speak. Not
a word, no explanation, the silence
moistened by his tears. The man who
could talk a mile a minute for hours
on end has been dead now for
thirty-six stone-cold years.

You wake from this dream and
and you wonder what he was
crying about, but you will
never know why
he spoke not a word.

MR. JONES [FOOTNOTE TO BOB DYLAN]

You don't know Mr. Jones
do you that the walls
you build to keep others
out will lock you in
to feed you fears
and shrink the horizon
of who you might be
to the disappearing
shadow of your best self.

Give Urizen enough rope
and he will tie his own
hands and feet
to fret himself away
in endless grief.

Build your walls,
imprison yourself,
feed your fears,
drown in your tears,
won't you,
Mr. Jones,
your very flesh
shrunk off your bones.

ALL OUR SHIPS HAVE SAILED

All our ships sailed away a long time ago.
Some were cruising yachts that
hit hidden rocks and sank into
the dark depths of the silent sea.
Some were bright brigantines that
glided far past our ken to blessed
isles we will never live to see.
Some were white-winged clippers
that ferried away our fondest
dreams. Some were great ocean liners
now long past their service date,
rusting on some forgotten pier
on a distant continent. Some
were container ships endlessly
crisscrossing the same seas,
delivering goods we never even
knew we had. Some were
catamarans trafficking between
coral reefs in search of something
we had lost over the years but
were hoping to recover.

All these our
ships left their harbor such a
long time ago and we will never
even know when it was that

they heaved anchor or what
distant shores they were sailing to.

UNLIKE LEAR

Rain, thunder, and lightning don't faze
me in the least. I walk through it,
tough-skinned old man that I've
become. A survivor, unlike that
foolish raging Lear, I don't implicate
the elements, or imprecate against them,
or hold them to account. I'm not deluded
in the least about the burden of our
naked humanity, nor how we prey
on each other for our mutual advantage.

Poor Tom, bare forked animal,
is the lowest common denominator
of what we've been and always will be.
The rich man lives at the expense of the poor,
and the female spreads her legs and takes
what she must because she knows she
has no choice.

                                        Brute history simply
repeats itself ad nauseam in every
corner of the world. No birds in a cage
know any of that, though blinded
men feeling their solitary way
learn in due time to accept what
fate dishes out to them. Age wise

and wizened, a weathered veteran I am,
willing to face what inevitably comes,
willing to take my chances on the
perpetual cosmic merry-go-round,
whistling my solitary songs in all
weathers and seasons as best I can.

A SIMPLE SCENE (LEIPZIG, MAY 2017)

Gingerly she holds and carries
the glasses of fruit juice to her smiling
parents and grandparents seated
at a table at the hotel breakfast
buffet. She makes several resolute
trips, serious at this task as only a
five- or six-year-old can be.

I watch
with wonder this little girl's
single-minded focus on this
simple task, performed with
all the purity of a communion ritual.
I see her here and now,
but also fifty years hence,
a middle-aged woman
performing other tasks
with none of the purity of
devotion of her juice journeys
this Sunday morning.

THE POPE'S REVENGE

An enormous Television Tower
looms over Berlin, built
to testify to the supremacy
of a misbegotten totalitarian
dream. While the workers
had to wait up to sixteen years
for that sardine-can travesty
of a car, The Trabi, the ruling elite
were chauffeured around in
Volvo limousines.

In Berlin
you can see that proud erection
everywhere, the ideological
index of a regime that had
a great fall when its misnamed
anti-fascist Wall came Humpty-
Dumptying down in 1989.

On a cloudless afternoon when
the sun hits the metal gleaming
bubble near the top of the Tower,
a large cross materializes
on its shining surface:
the Pope's Revenge the locals
call it. Or maybe it's just
Jesus getting one over on Marx.

FOR ROBBIE
[WHO DEPARTED THIS WORLD ON JULY 5, 2017]

The walls haunt us with their silence,
the large house is hollowed out.
Already it seems eons since
we held you a mere four days ago
as you strained against my
caressing hands to get back up
from the floor of the vet's
antiseptic cubicle until
the needle found a vein
in your leg and the death
potion stopped your loving heart
as I felt your last breaths.

In your nearly thirteen
years with us you filled
every crevice of our lives.
You were the shadow and
reflex of our good days
and our bad, of our laughter
and our tears. You shared
yourself with us without
reserve even as your playful
energy and majestic strength
began to falter and give out.

You bore your pain without
complaint, the canine fortitude
infused into your very bones.
Up to your final day you went
with us on our long walks
in our woods that now will
never be quite the same for
us without you. Your pillow is
still in your room; the half-
empty treat jars, the food
and water bowl. We can't
bear to remove them yet,
sad signifiers of the demise
of our sweet Boy, Robbie the
Weimaraner, whose absence weighs
us down with the rich burden
of the years and lives we shared.

I HEARD THE CRACK

I heard the bones in your ankle
crack when you slipped on a wet root
as you walked briskly behind me on
the path down to the gully that we cross
on our daily hikes in our woods.

A simple twist of fate
turned our lives upside down
in an instant. Despite all those
long walks your bones are weak,
the surgeon said, describing
a complex procedure to repair
the compound fracture. If
you were twenty years old,
he said, I'd put some more
pins in there, but your bones
aren't up to it. "Satisfactory"
given your age and the state of
your bones was the best he could
offer on that follow-up visit ten days
after surgery.

Now you're laid
up for at least eight weeks,
with no pressure allowed on
the injured leg, using a walker,

crutches, and a knee scooter
to get around. Friends have
brought food and cheer,
but there's little comfort
in our fears about when
and how well that ankle
will heal, and whether you
will ever stride again through
woods and fields as we have
done for so many years.

As for playing tennis again,
that may just be a distant
dream, even as the new racquet
you bought a week before
your fall and that you got
to use only once sulks in a
dark corner of the hall closet.

But *hope is that thing with feathers*,
and the phoebe perched on
a chair on the deck looking
through the window at you
in bed with your leg propped up
on pillows intimates as much.

WHY?

Stop asking the *why* question
you've been asking all your life.
It's stupid and pointless.

Listen to the language of leaves.
Feel the raindrops in your face.
Watch TV. Play tennis. Mow
the lawn. Shovel the snow.
Eat your pizza. Walk your dog.

EGO

Ego is so hard to let go
of. Wherever you go
it's always ego.

As you get older
it shouldn't be so hard
to let go of that
old battered ego.

If you could let go
what would you know
without your ego?

Just who or what
would you be
ego-free?

Could you ever assay
that state? And
what would be your fate?

Stripped of ego
how could you show
who you are?

You've come so far
but are you willing today
to throw that old ego away?

VOYAGER

On and on I voyage ad infinitum
through the icy silence of the vast
continuum of interstellar space,
the last remnant of the home
and the star I left behind many
millions of years ago.

As I pushed through the envelope
of the solar system the planets
were diminishing spots of light
in the retrospect of my cameras,
the earth a distant dot on
the verge of vanishing.

On and on I travel.
My sensors and circuits have
long been dead, but the eternal
heart of the thing I still am as I speed
between the galaxies is a grooved
golden record containing an
encyclopedic compendium of
the world and the life of the species
that brought me into being and
sent me on my endless solitary
journey through the vast empty
expanses of the universe.

MONKEY GOD

The orange monkey tweets and yaps
while all his followers clap and clap.
He promises them the moon
but delivers only empty fumes.

This gross god who struts and spouts on the stage
embodies all the corruptions of a fallen age.
While he stuffs his face with chocolate cake
he knows he's just a loud and sinister fake.
Someday this bloated balloon will surely burst,
but in the meantime we have to fear the worst.
When the Monkey God runs the show
those who have no shame are in the know.
The rest of us can only hope and pray
that this gross nightmare will soon pass away.

TWO TINY CHIRPS

Two tiny chirps recently registered
the cosmic waves of time-space curvature
caused by the collision of two of the
largest objects in our universe:
binary massive black holes.

There are hundreds of billions
of stars in our Milky Way Galaxy,
and hundreds of billions of galaxies
in our universe, and our universe
may be only one among many.

The neural networks inside our skulls
have begun to sort all this out,
as our grey matter has begun
to map the remotest galaxies
and the background radiation
of the Big Bang as well as

The magical mysteries of the
subatomic particles with those
weird names that keep on
multiplying and confounding
some of the laws of physics that
we thought we'd pinned down.

And just when we will have succeeded
in formulating the Theory of Everything,
most species on this planet will become
extinct, and we too will face our end
knowing full well the havoc that we've
wreaked on an earth that we have
made increasingly a living hell.

HEALING [FOR ELSJE]

If touch alone could heal
I would heal you back to health.
Of the many ways our bodies
can betray us, the bitter bone ache
and sore joints of rheumatoid arthritis
is only one.

            I wish my touch
could be like the warming
early spring breezes that blow
the first flowers of the season
into bloom. I wish my touch
could take away the pain
and make you whole again.

I wish I could heal you into
the very lithe and limber
frolicking of the spotted
fawns as they chase around
the pond and jump and
frisk on our back lawn.
Oh, if only wishing could
make it so!

THE QUESTION

We're condemned to live our entire
lives not knowing the miracle
we are living. Our very being
here may be the answer
to a question that we can
never ever know how to ask.

Nevertheless we try,
never knowing what
the right questions might
be to get us to the one
that we're the answer to.

NOTRE DAME DE PARIS, APRIL 15, 2019

Our Lady of Sorrow, our Lady of perennial Hope,
Queen of humanity's highest thoughts,
your great church is in flames,
your celestial and majestic soaring edifice
on the Island of the City is
for now an empty smoking ruin
that moves us all to tears,
but that will be rebuilt anew
in splendor to inspire countless
generations to come.

But You
preside unharmed, ethereal
and immaterial as the forever
Queen of suffering and aspiring
human hearts the whole world
over, Lady of our Sorrows,
Lady of perennial Hope, Queen
of the ancient city by the Seine,
Notre Dame de Paris.

HOW NOT TO GET OFF A SKI LIFT

You chat with the two strangers riding
with you. When they push off
the lift chair on the platform
at the top, you're inattentive
until the ground rapidly falls
away. As you rise up high
into the air, you make a split-
second decision to jump
off the lift, crash landing
very hard on your right side.

You're stunned almost into oblivion.
Bravo! you've done it!
And you haven't even broken
your hip, the X-rays reveal
the next day when you can't
walk without crutches or a
walker. So what you've got now,
as you hobble about in pain
for weeks, is the sheer pleasure
of bragging rights: how not
to get off the fucking ski lift.
If you want to know that,
hey, I'm your man.

PROSPERO RETIRED

Back in Milan I am once more,
withdrawn into my library with
all my books for company.
As for the conjuring, I'm done
with that for good.
Ferdinand and Miranda
rule the dukedom now,
while my wayward and
resentful brother skulks
about the palace. There's no
Ariel here to keep an eye
on him. That airy sprite is
now gone into thin air.

I do not miss the island that was
a refuge to castaway me and
the child who was my sole
concern until that heathen
creature Caliban showed up
to do us menial services.
Ungrateful and treasonous
wretch that he was entering
into league with some of
the crew whose shipwreck I
orchestrated with my so
magical and potent art.

I taught him how to speak
and meant to humanize him
until he sought to break
Miranda's virgin knot.
I made him pay a heavy price
for that, vile slave that he
is and always will be.
But now he's left behind
all alone, unaccommodated,
undone as his own master on
a barren and deserted isle,
while I dream my bookish dreams
here at the quiet tail end of
my so reclusive and retired life.

MIRANDA IN MILAN

Here in Milan this new world
isn't quite so brave any more.
My uncle that villain keeps
ogling me when no one is
looking, trying to back me
into dark corners. And my Prince
Charming wanted a society
wedding. My billowing white
gown was ordered from Paris,
the train held up by six
simpering chambermaids.

I, who never had a clue about
the way of the world, am
now swimming in it, trying
to keep my head above water.
The other day when I caught
Ferdie pinching the rear of one
of my maids, he only laughed and
and said it was the custom here.
He also spent a duke's ransom
hiring some Englishman,
Inigo by name, to orchestrate
what they call a wedding masque.

Once ignorant as a rock
I'm starting to find my way
in this strange new world.
My father is back in his library
lost in his books, while I'm
getting the hang of what's
what here in this my new high-
society life. But at night I
still have dreams of the island
and the starry silence
of those distant seas.

ANTONIO ON THE REBOUND

It was my pleasure to depose him,
and cast him and that silly brat
my niece adrift upon the seas.
It would have been better
to dispatch them, but that old
ass the councilor Gonzalo used
his influence at court for
a mere sentence of exile.

Prospero, so infatuated with his
library, was utterly unfit to rule.
But he survived to shipwreck
and torture me with delusions
of the most awful kind. And then
his pardoning me was the worst
offense of all. Having to be
forever in his debt is simply
unbearable. Now he's back
to his old ways with his nose
perpetually in his books.
And his brat has ripened into
quite the saucy Milanese miss,
hot to trot with Ferdinand
and show her face at court.

All I can do for now is bide my
my time until I can choke him
with one of his moth-eaten tomes.
Mr. Party Boy Ferdinand should
be easy enough to dispatch.
Sebastian is already in the know,
just waiting for my signal to
launch me into my second reign.

ARIEL FREE

Where the bee sucks
there suck I, from pole
to pole I can fly
in the blinking of an eye.
It was very fine of him
to free me from
the cloven pine,
fixed there by that
foul witch Sycorax,
though how an airy
spirit like me could be
forced into a tree
is certainly a great mystery.

But now again free I am
to the elements,
free as the air to waft
wherever I care.
He made the pine gape
so I could serve him
as the invisible helpmate
of his magic spells.
Once released from
that tree, my invisible
agency helped him
to regain his dukedom
beyond the sea.

That feat achieved, he
let me go to indulge
my own flighty delights,
here, there, and everywhere,
ethereal and mysterious
creature of the air that I am,
subject now again to no
power but mine own
wayward delights
both day and night,
in sunshine and in rain.
Yes, now again I can.

FALLUJAH, 2004

In a pitch-black room in a bomb-ravaged
house we shadows fought without even
seeing each other. I taunted him,
Infidel dog I will cut off your head and
take your dog tags. The blades of our
knives, fist-clenched, flashed in the dark.

My hand found his hair but as I
yanked back his head his blade
found me and pushed deep inside.
My grip slackened and my fingers
slid down his face as they caressed
his cheek. With my last breath I
forgave him his bloody deed,
brothers now in an unforgiving
world run by the ciphers who sit
behind desks while we soldier
victims of enemy camps expire
in the muck and the mire
of their flatulent dreams.

JESUS

Unlike some of his professed followers
so many centuries later, Jesus was
an itinerant preacher seeking to turn
the established order upside down.
He asked the children to approach
but unlike some of his shepherds
and ministers pretending to spread
his gospel the world over he
didn't welcome them only to
to prey upon and abuse them.

Unlike the rich and the powerful
who have mostly run a corrupt
world strictly for their own benefit,
he spoke for the poor, the dispossessed,
and the outcast. He didn't kowtow to
the wealthy, and he wasn't loath
to call them out, the money lenders
in the temple, those fat camels
eyeing the needle's eye of profit.

He didn't live in a palace or sit
in a limousine like some of his
pompously bedecked false avatars,
but rode to Jerusalem on an ass.

His father's kingdom was a generous
figment of his fervent imagination,
but he also knew that this celestial
realm was a glorious vision that would
forever change the world, and that
all the pharisaic hypocrisies of his
professed followers cannot entirely
obscure: his dream kingdom
glittering like the distant stars
on a clear and cloudless night.

LATE JULY MONARCH

A monarch butterfly fluttered by,
lighter than a feather dancing in
the air. The morning sky was bright
blue, and the midsummer green
was everywhere. The butterfly
made a few orange-winged passes,
and then vanished like a
seasonal ghost. As long as
there are still some monarchs
dancing on the late July air
there is some hope for a troubled
world so full of grief and care.

THAT BRIGHT BUBBLE

When that bright bubble Hope
bursts in the air
don't give in to despair
but simply dare
to venture something new.

Let Blake and Dickinson
inspire you who were mostly
unknown in their day
but whose names today
live on in a posthumous fame,
whose career of glory
is a well-known story.

But to wish for such fame
is surely a losing game
and yet another version of that Bubble
that causes so many mortals
so much trouble.

TURNING SEVENTY-SIX [AUGUST 18, 2019]

So today I turned seventy-six.
Is that good news, or bad?
Well, the good news is that
I'm still alive. And the bad?
That that Grim Reaper
is inevitably creeping closer
and closer. But that's as it
should be for me, a mere
member of the human family.

We know our story always
has a beginning as well as an end.
As the former recedes into
the far distance of a country
almost lost to memory,
the latter awaits us, as yet
invisible and unknowable.
I'm fine with that, for now
at least, as I welcome
the days and years (I hope)
to come. Through my long
life I've learned to love both
a rising and a setting sun.

Everything and Nothing

EVERYTHING

Like the clouds
and the wind
and the leaves
and the snowflakes
and the tides
and night and day
and the seasons
and the stars and galaxies
everything comes and goes.
And so do we.
It's as simple as that.
And as complicated and as cruel and as glorious and as perennial as that.
Take it for what it is and for what it isn't.
Period.

SEPTEMBER WINDS [SEPTEMBER 14, 2019]

September winds are soughing through
the trees. Already green leaves litter
the ground. The goldenrod are in their
full golden flush, and an occasional
monarch butterfly wings the casual air.
The coming season is in the offing.
It's almost already here—again.

After the night rain and clouds
obscured the full harvest moon
today the bright late summer sun
is drying the wet grass and beginning
to season the profusion of leaves
still on the trees for their chromatic
charade of mid-autumn glory.

THE PAST

The past is a foreign country
that changes as you change.
No tourist visa will get you there.
As you approach the horizon
of who you were recedes
into the far distance.

The buildings you knew
have dematerialized.
What you think you can reach
has dissolved into thin air.
The past you once knew
has flown the coop.

The once-familiar faces
and places are gone or strangely
altered. And so are you
from whoever you once were.
When you try to touch the past
you find there's simply nothing there.
Even the fissures in your face
are undecipherable hieroglyphs
you seek in vain to read.

GOLDEN OCTOBER DAYS

Now more so than ever I relish
Those golden-toned October days
when the leaves turn yellow
and glimmer with dewdrops
in the early morning sun.

It's a season poised between
the heat of summer and the chill
of deep winter when the landscape
can assume a special kind of
crystalline clarity whose soothing
radiance lets us know that even
though the better part of the year
has flown away we can still find
a quiet kind of peace of mind
in those glowing golden days
before the coming of the season's
end and the inevitable arrival
of winter's long deep freeze.

COLIN CLOUT'S COME HOME AGAIN—NOT

After more than four centuries or so
Spenser's shepherd from long ago
has come back from a deep sleep again
to tend his flock in sunshine and rain.
Chief of the sylvan poet singers was he,
who could play a lovely melody
fingering his oaten flute so free.

But now well into the new millennium
Colin no longer feels at all at home,
for not only is he all alone,
but the meadows and pastures he knew so well
have basically all gone straight to hell.
Some to parking lots, some to buildings so tall
Colin can't see the sky at all.

And a summer heat so extreme
it wants to make Colin scream
instead of singing his country songs.
The globe's been hotting up for so long
and poor Colin simply can't fathom what's going on.
What fields are left are parched and scorched,
and our shepherd poet feels like his brain's been torched.

AUTUMN LEAVES

Every wind-blown drifting autumn leaf
is like a life that's been lived:
one of a kind and unique in its configuration,
but also typical and generic,
one of many many millions.

Like these leaves we come and go,
from the dawn of our first spring
to our last fall that will strip us down
and leave us on the ground
to be reabsorbed into
the greater realm of being.

Our brief leaf lives soon enough
are mere ancient history,
lost to posterity, atoms
merged again into the
perennial dance of
the stars and galaxies.

LIFE LINES

Conventional lives follow regular and straight paths
that can easily be charted by simple graphs.
They can be those of athlete celebrities
as well as non-descript mediocrities.
Some lives are strictly circular and end
where they began the course they ran
and I'm not quite sure what these portend.
Perhaps there's a measure of wisdom won
by the time such circles have been run.

Nabokov preferred to think of his life as an
upward moving spiral transcending exile and strife,
a series of quasi-Hegelian swerves
synthetic and much more subtle than simple curves.

Looking back on the elongating line of my later years,
having pacified if not conquered myriad fears
I don't discern a straight line or simple round
or even spiral, but what I think I've found
is this: a sort of zig-zagging tapestry,
with a zig here and a zag there,
seeming to lead at once nowhere and everywhere.
And that's the graph, such as it is, of my drawn-out identity:
An ultimately ungraspable and ungraphable me.

IN THE AGE OF TRUMP

The Idiot Wind rules today.
Truth is disposable or dismissed as fake news.
Bread and circuses are updated for the age
of the internet and spread on Twitter
and Facebook. He's taken up residence
in our heads without paying any rent
and even if he's successfully
impeached, we still won't be able
to evict him. He's simply and unremittingly
everywhere all the time and
we can't get a break from him
thanks to the perpetual media storm.

A Bloated Bag of Mendacity
and self-promoting Mediocrity
looms over our media-bombarded days
and nights, and for now we simply
cannot get away from
this unremitting blight.

MAYBE

I want to write a poem, but I don't
know about what: maybe everything
and maybe nothing. Maybe the snowflakes
drifting like downy feathers past
my study window, quietly now
after the early November snowstorm
during the night. Maybe my long
walk with Theo the rescue dog
in the woods, my boots plowing
through the deep snow and
Theo cavorting with fallen
branches like a little maniac?

Maybe about being retired and
safely withdrawn from the whirl
of the world, reflecting and
observing its myriad corruptions
in places both high and low
so it always seems the Same Old
Same Old here below?

Maybe about the incomprehensible
and inexplicable mystery of how
the human brain over billions
of years could evolve out of
stardust? Or maybe only about
what I should have for lunch.

FORTUNA

Fortuna, that wanton pagan goddess
who slowly turns her great wheel
granting some more, and some much less
and causing everywhere and always a good deal
of consternation and confusion,
likes to lift up the vaingloriously rotten
of every town and nation
with their corrupt and ill-gotten
gains and unearned renown,
only to bring them back down
in the course of its inevitable revolution
and prostrate them on the ground,
their names covered
with ignominy and shame
and with no one to blame
for their downfall's stench
but themselves and that
capricious Roman wench.

EVERYTHING AND NOTHING

Everything and *nothing* are words we use
every day, but we can't really *think* them.
The idea of "everything" is ultimately
one degree beyond the outer reaches
of Infinity. And "nothing" is just as
much beyond our conceptual capacity.

If we stretch our minds far enough
we can think of pure empty space,
and we can imagine it shrinking
until it's almost a single point,
but beyond that our minds
simply cannot ever reach.

So "nothing," like "everything,"
is something we can easily say
but something we can never ever
really *know*.

IT'S OKAY, YOU SAY

At a certain late point in your life you say
with a certain shrug of resignation,
It's okay.

It's okay that autocrats and their corrupt
cronies are running the show
in many parts of the world.
It's okay that desperate refugees are
drowning at sea. It's okay that
the globe continues to warm.
It's okay that children at the Mexican
border are separated from their parents
and put into dismal detention pens.
It's okay that Big Pharma executives
hold whole countries hostage
with hugely inflated prices,
and that legal drug-dealing
billionaires have addicted millions
to opioids. It's okay that drug
cartels run rampant. And it's okay
that the poor and downtrodden
often only have Jesus to appeal to
as their last hope and resort,
and that rotten politicians and
their cynical enablers and herd-
like deluded followers invoke him
for their nefarious ends.

It's okay, you say,
and shrug your shoulders,
even though you know damn well
that these things and many others
can never ever be okay.

THE MYSTERY

All our lives long we live it.
Those pinpoints of bright
light in a clear night sky,
the stars, are its neural
network. But that network is
also in us. And if the Mystery is
a long dark tunnel, we hope
against hope that there is
a light at the end of it.

But we can't know, and the
more we read the less we
know. And the more we think
the greater that Mystery is.

The longer we are in it and
it is in us, the less we recall
that it is also a daily wonder,
a sheer miracle that we first
beheld with the dawning of our
consciousness. As we move with
the tides of time the wonder mostly
fades away in the mere pedestrian
routine of our busy days
even as the Mystery endures.

THE INTERIOR LIFE

The interior life is a psychic black hole
suffused by mysterious and radiant
surprises. We now know that at
the quantum level it's interfused
with the universe in ways we
have not yet begun to fathom.

For far too many now that inner
world is less and less accessible
because of the relentless and
unceasing noise of the outer
world bearing down on us
with a blubber whale's weight.

Ask a meditating monk for
a mere hint of how you might
begin to access those so
deep down magical depths
within that too many now
entirely ignore at their peril.

The idiot wind of that shrill outer
world blows us further and further
from what is so deep within us
so that we may never even get
a hint to know no matter how long
a surface life we may end up living.

VERBAL DIFFERENCES

If you don't know the difference
between a *combine* and a *concubine*
you may be a bit of a moron.
If you know the difference between
a *gnome* and a *gnomon*
you're more literate than most
and maybe even a bit of a nerd.
If you don't know the difference
between *prostate* and *prostrate*,
or *lie* and *lay*, or *affect* and *effect*
or even *principal* and *principle*
you're just part of the common herd
that doesn't honor the integrity of the word.
And if you don't know the difference
between *there* and *their*
and *who's* and *whose*
you can drive some of us to despair.
But if you do know the difference
Between *rein* and *reign*
you've redeemed yourself again.
As for the difference between *it's* and *its*
I leave that to more accomplished wits.

HALL OF MIRRORS

Located in the hills and woods above Hemlock Lake
here I in my mid-seventies,
my thoughts are sifted and framed
by the perennial cycle of the seasons
and the daily passing of our lives.

Retired in this rural retreat,
a mere pensioner of my own time,
I observe the ways of this too-busy world
and the natural disasters and human follies
and crimes that are the burden of the daily
news. And I have too much to say, and
nothing at all to myself or anyone
else about all this. It's too easy to take
cheap shots on the sidelines or even to
offer up our penny's worth of wisdom
when we've reached a certain silver age.

I'm no sage, but perhaps my sight lines
are clearer than those of the ones caught up
in the midst of the fray, but then too much
thinking about what's wrong with the world
can simply lead me astray. I try to defer
or suspend judgment; I'm not on a Grand
Jury judging our world's derelictions.

Age confers no privileged perspectives
per se to serve as nostrums for a fallen world,
even if it does allow us to catch occasional
glimpses of the hall of distorting mirrors
in which most of us spend most of
the days of our lives.

DESPAIR AND HOPE (DECEMBER 26, 2019)

The calm still lingers in the quiet
of the sky the day after the child
in the manger was born among strangers.
We all come into the world as strangers,
but most of us are welcomed into families.
Yet so many now are refugees in an
unwelcoming and alien world.

The human family today is fractured
beyond repair in so many places.
The infant in the stable's cradle
has figured hope and home for lost
souls and refugees of broken lives
for two thousand plus years.

Hope knows no limits in either time
or space, unlike despair, which cannot
pass beyond a certain point, but must
suffocate in its own poisoned air.

Hope fuels dreams, and dreams
carry lives and sustain them in
spheres undreamt of by those whose
lives and minds cannot reach beyond
the mere exigencies of a material world.

In the quiet of a late December day
the calm still lingers in the balance
of hope and despair.

NEW DECADE (DECEMBER 28, 2019]

A new year, a new decade
are just around the corner.
And I'm in the second half of my seventies.
What will the 2020s bring us?
More global warming with consequences
both foreseen and unforeseen?

More new wars and long-standing
ones continued? More people
dislocated by the millions?
More demagogues fueling
the fires of discontent?

Will the doves of peace have to
fly above increasingly troubled
waters, their wings stripped
above storm-tossed seas?
The new decade looms large in
our questioning and troubled minds.

JANUARY 1, 2020

It's just another grey-sky day here
at the beginning of a new decade.
Nature doesn't keep calendars,
but works by seasonal cycles.

Ask the stars who bear silent witness
to the passing millennia. A new
decade isn't even a blink of an
eye or a grain of sand in the grand
cosmic sea of time and space.

The universe doesn't keep calendars.
Only we do so, compulsively
observing the days, months, and
seasons come and go. We count
and number our forever fleeting
lives, knowing the odds are against
us even if we can never know
the final count.

HIDDEN LANGUAGES

Approaching my ninth decade
I've read many books and learned
several languages. But in all
these years I've never learned
the language of trees,
the language of flowers,
the language of birds.

All of these are connected
by unnumbered hidden filaments
to our lives, interwoven with them
in most mysterious and magical ways.
They tell us things we do not know.
Perhaps in my eighties I can also
learn to understand what they may
have to say that I've ignored
my whole life long.

ROT

"Rot itself is life; there is more living tissue . . . in a fallen tree than in a living one. . . . Life and death are literally interconnected here."

The hidden networks connecting the trees
in the soil are something we don't ever see,
but the scientists tell us these interact in a
constant relationship of growth and decay.

Our lives as well are defined by the processes
of ripening and rotting, until the former
diminishes and the latter gains the ascendancy.
Our planet too undergoes such endless cycles
of protracted growth and decay.

But now in the age of the Anthropocene
what we're coming to see more and more
is that we've put our hand in the balance
of these perennial processes, blighting
biodiversity, forcing an increasing number
of species into sheer extinction.

We who thought we were the masters
of the natural world commanding it
to do our unceasing bidding are now
heading for disasters of our own making,
so that more and more of the teeming
life on our planet will disappear.

And now already those who are least
at fault are paying the price of a
warming planet: Kangaroos and
koalas scorched by brush fires,
and desperate polar bears looking
lost and forlorn on drifting floes of ice.

SURFACES ARE SAFE

Surfaces are safe, most people think,
so they choose to stay on the surface.

Depths are dark and dangerous, they think,
depths are danger zones that
you enter and venture on
all alone and on your own.
And so they avoid them at all cost.

Down there are the shadows
of primal forms that sometimes
haunt us in our dreams
and hidden scenes we would
rather not bear witness to.

But what is lost in the long run
by staying on the surface is
who and what we are
or might have been.
Surfaces are safe, yes,
like prisons are safe.

INDIAN SUMMER IN MID-JANUARY

Indian Summer in January is an oxymoron,
but that's what we've had for several days
now before the rites of winter return
in full force. If this is also a rare benefit
of global warming, we're happy to take it
as one of life's unexpected surprises.
Indian Summer in mid-January may
be unprecedented, but then we're
living in unprecedented times
when all kinds of developments are
occurring that aren't supposed to.
And Indian Summer in January is
most likely the least of these.

THE LEGIONNAIRE OF LIES

He lives and breathes by lying.
He's a living lie. His lies are legion.
He's the Legionnaire of Lies.
If he were Pinocchio his nose
would be long enough to wind
around the outer reaches of
the solar system and then some.

The swarming host of his big fibs is
like another biblical plague,
locusts covering the sky as far
as the eye can see, devastating
any budding crop of good sense,
of honesty and decency and rectitude.

His lies fill the air like a noxious
gas that makes us choke and
puke. His lies are everywhere
for he is the Legionnaire of Lies.

THE SELF IS?

The self is hateful, some French
sage said several hundred years
ago. But we've also heard the
praise of self-reliance from
a host of other sages.

More recently some have
asserted in full hubris that
there is no self, the word
itself an empty signifier.

But maybe when push comes
to shove our single and singular
self is pretty much all we've got—
and all we've joined with it,
and taken in, and all we've
ever said and done and been.

SNOWFLAKES [JANUARY 19]

Snowflakes are whirling past my window
every which way. Today is a white
midwinter day. I saw the same flakes
as a child so very many years ago.

Snowflakes don't ever seem to change,
only we do. So I can't quite see
them the same way I once did.
But I still enjoy their white whirling
sameness almost as much as I used to.

PLAY

The most essential and defining human activity
is nothing else but play.
When we can make work play,
we can make work pay.

But when we turn play into work
and nothing but work
then our human essence
drains away,
and we shirk what
we're meant to be,
to become mere appendages
of a mechanical and inhuman world.

Play is the very thing
that makes us take wing
and our hearts sing.

LOVE IS

Love is not wanting you young again,
but sharing
or even bearing
all of your pain.

HOW MANY TRILLIONS?

If there are at least one hundred billion
galaxies in the observable universe,
and if there are at least one hundred billion
stars in ours, the Milky Way, then
there are at least how many stars
in our universe? And if most
stars have orbiting planets,
then how many planets?

Well, you do the math.
But whatever the final figure, the
billions turned into many trillions,
how credible is it really to think
that there might be some sort of
divine cosmic presence keeping
an eye on you and me and all
the little contentious people
on our little out-of-the-way
and pedestrian planet?

"CAN THE EARTH BE SWALLOWED BY A BLACK HOLE?"

Asks a young astronomer. The question
is mostly a rhetorical attention grabber,
but the possibility, no matter how
infinitesimally remote, is intriguing
nevertheless. Given the shape our
planet is in due to what we've done
to it in the age of the Anthropocene
and how we continue to ravage
and savage it, it might very well seem
an appropriate final cosmic act
to bring down the curtain
on this dismal terrestrial scene.

SURVEILLANCE CAPITALISM

"[There is] a new economic logic that I call 'surveillance capitalism.' Its success depends upon one-way-mirror operations engineered for our ignorance and wrapped in a fog of misdirection, euphemism and mendacity."—Shoshana Zuboff

We all know about the Robber Barons of the Gilded Age,
and we're happy to know that long ago we turned the page
on those voracious and legally sanctioned crooks.
We've also known about the dangers of big government
as our benevolent Big Brother that spies on us and looks
at all we're doing. But now a more sinister threat has arisen:
Surveillance Capitalism. Those young computer and internet
nerds who seemed heaven-sent due to our naïve misprision,
they who run and rake in billions at Amazon and Facebook and Google
treat the world's countries as their private little poodle
whose tail they can wag at their will. They suck up our all
information online, as we've discovered to our consternation,
like giant vacuum cleaners with hidden but immense power,
twenty-four/seven minute by minute and hour by hour
to manipulate us without our even suspecting or knowing.

There's Zuckerberg at Facebook who's always showing
such a kind and benign demeanor with his boyish face,
and Bezos the founder of Amazon to whose eternal disgrace
his harried robot factory workers constitute a new slave class.

At Google that sleek Indian computer Wunderkind Sundar Pichai
is just as crass with his totalitarian dream of A.I.
silently and invisibly running the world from the Cloud in the Sky,
with none to discern the drawn-out death of democracy.

The new digital Robber Barons of the twenty-first century
are not so crass as the old ones of the infamous Gilded Age
but their nefarious and global secret surveillance schemes
are more than enough to turn into nightmares our waking dreams.

THE VOICES OF THE DEAD

Once you are in your advanced years
you can hear the voices of the dead all
around you. You see their faces
in the strangest of places
mirroring their lost lives.

They whisper to you in your
dreams, those long echo chambers
of the distant past when they were
still near and dear to you.

The dead surround you like
a halo or a shroud. They connect
you to who and what you've been
and still are like invisible
threads spun out to infinity.

LIVING VOICES

These days we hear too many voices,
voices like whirlpools that make
our heads spin. Impassioned voices
that spout sheer nonsense and pass
it off as purest sense. And voices
that wind and wing and buzz about our
ears like demented siren songs that lead
only to the dead end of a quagmire.

Strident and presumptuous voices
of fools parading as experts
and blindly serving the interests
of a labyrinth of hidden powers.

Insistent voices that drive us to
distraction, voices that ricochet
in our media-addled and besotted
brains, so many voices, so that all we
seek for sheer relief is nothing else but
a soundproofed inner sanctum of silence,
a quiet room humming to the metronome
of the steady beating of our hearts.

DIE LÜGENPRESSE

The lying press, Hitler infamously called it,
though he's the one who specialized
in the Big Lie. A press that's free is
supposed to be the bulwark of
democracy. But the press in fact
often distorts the news it claims
only to report for its own money-
making ends: it chases sensation
and celebrity; the death of a sports
star or an actor is spun as a world-
shaking loss, while the daily lives
of the vast majority are glossed
over as unprintable dross.

The daily news thrives on disasters,
tragedies, and scandals; good news
hardly earns a headline or even a byline;
murder, corruption, and crime are
its favorite daily fare, and sexual
derelictions brought to light,
especially those of the high and
mighty, are its regular fodder.

What good ordinary people
do every day gets little or no
media play. The press lies not

so much as it distorts the world
it purports to cover for its own
particular profiteering ends.

THE CREATURES SUFFER

The creatures suffer. They have
suffered for thousands upon thousands
of years our impositions upon them.
We clothe ourselves in them.
We enslave them. We eat them.
We destroy their habitats for
our domineering purposes.

Daily they suffer our unthinking
and self-righteous cruelties.
They bear the yoke and live in
the pain of our self-appointed
mastery and the manifold delusions
of our unceasing and barbaric hegemony.
The creatures suffer and suffer.

WE WEAR THE MASK

We wear the mask.
It started in Asia with people
wearing masks to filter out
the polluted air. We saw them
in markets, in subways,
and in airports. But now we
too wear them to protect
ourselves from the filthy
poison we spew at each other
day in and day out. So
we too now put on the mask,
that thin white divider
between our worst selves.

SEALED DREAM

When you're in a nightmare you
can't wake up from,
what do you do?

When you open your eyes
but you're still in it
where can you go?

When there's no escape
from this sealed dream
what's left for you to do?

Is there another universe
to escape to?
Could that ever be true?

CORONA, FOR NOW

We walk the paths in our woods,
we watch the wind sweep in waves
across the surface of our pond,
and nothing seems to have changed,
but everything has changed:

Corona, Corona, Corona
ubiquitous and invisible,
you who haunt the news like
a bad dream that we can't
wake from. The politicians
talk and talk as you wash across
the globe. Brave souls in masks
and gowns, soldiers battling
on the front lines seek to
contain you, seek to save
the multitude of the stricken.

And we walk in our woods,
we watch the wind-rippled pond,
and we think nothing has
changed, even when we know
that everything has changed.
Corona, Corona, for now.

THINGS BROKEN

Sometimes things that are broken
can't be unbroken;
sometimes words that are spoken
can't be unspoken.

Sometimes wounds don't heal,
they just fester and fester.
Sometimes the dreams we've chased
for the length of a long lifetime have crossed
the line of the event horizon
and can never be recalled or replaced.

Sometimes the very things that are broken
are the fragments that we shore up
against the ruins of our lives,
and sometimes it's our forever-
unspoken words that we leave
and that no one can hear or see
as our last will and lasting legacy.

COVID TIME

The days and weeks bleed into each other.
The ordinary routines weigh down
on us. But these aren't ordinary times
to say the least. We must learn
to do with less, like in a war.
But we don't exactly know who
or what it is we're fighting.

I take my daily walks.
I watch the news compulsively.
I sleep longer and have more
nightmares. I'm more tired
and irritable. Time seems to
drag and drag. When will this all
end, and what will be the new
normal, we all wonder.
The days merge like the test
patterns on a television screen.

PANDEMIC DAYS

In these pandemic days
time slows. It oozes
like molasses. It drags
out the hours. I try
to flatten the curve.
I stay at home. I go
to bed at eight. I read
A Journal of the Plague Year
and note some of
the coincidences:

The infection spreading
like a raging wildfire,
the rich fleeing the cities,
businesses grinding to
a halt, shops shuttered,
the streets mostly empty,
the working people, living
from paycheck to paycheck
now without a paycheck
and desperate to get by,
the peddlers of fake cures,
the rising number of the dead
until the peak is passed
and time begins to resume
a semblance of its
ordinary course.

WORDS

Words can be bullets,
or they can be butterflies.
It's always our choice to
make with open eyes.
I leave the difference
between them
to the gentle and the wise.

DEEPWATER POET

He is our first deep water poet
the professor announced more
than six decades ago. He was
lecturing on John Masefield, who
famously expressed his wish
to go down to the sea again.

My professor must have forgotten
about *The Tempest* with its "full
fathom five thy father lies."
Almost everyone still knows
that play, but sea-singing
Masefield's fame has now
mostly faded, his laureate leaves
withered and his yellowing
pages largely unread.

But I do like the idea of a deep
water poet, diving into the depths
to search for the mermaids he
had glimpsed in his dreams.

A deep water poet searching down
in those dark and salty depths
could do this much and so much
more the deeper he dove and
the further away from shore.

I CAN'T BREATHE

Knee on neck, and not a
trace of concern or caring.
I can't breathe,
as fellow uniforms stand by
with not an iota of urgency.

I can't breathe:
one particular black man
on the ground, one particular
white police officer's knee
pressing down on his neck,
choking him to death.

For millennia these cruel
rituals of a world that doesn't
care to care, knees perpetually
on prostrated necks, has been
the norm. These uniforms
watching a prostrate black
man expire without moving
a finger are mere functionaries
in an age-old system of blood
sacrifice for whom the pleas of
I can't breathe will never
trouble their casual indifference.

But like small tapers in
a great and bloody night,
there always are a few
bystanders who speak up
and even act in protest,
sometimes at the risk of
their very lives. And perhaps
it's those tiny sparks who make
the most humane and saving
difference in a seemingly
forever-indifferent world and
who can cast a great light so
that we can all breathe again.

JOURNEY'S END

He hoped that at the end of his
journey it would be a sunny day,
followed by a clear starry night.

And he hoped that he'd managed to say
whatever it was he had to say,
and that he hadn't managed
to overstay his stay in a world
that grew more strange and puzzling
to him with every passing day.

And finally he hoped that despite
all his many flaws and errant ways
he'd managed to get a few things right.

TO GO GENTLE AND QUIET [AN ANSWER TO DYLAN THOMAS]

I hope to go gentle and quiet into that long dark night
when I finally reach the end of my winding road;
I know only too well that there's no point to putting up a fight
against the inevitability of my leave-taking and flight;
I leave it to the young who have to die before
their time to rage and fight; as for me and my
aging ilk whose chosen sign is the setting sun
and the quiet pleasures and gnawing aches of old
age, going quiet and gentle into that good night
after a long life sounds, well, just about right.

NOTHING

Speak again, nothing will come of nothing.

Well yes, you try to say everything and
then end up saying nothing. But
nothing's okay sometimes when
everything is simply beyond your reach.
And nothing lasts forever.

You say what you can, and you do
what you can. Which isn't much
for sure. Doors open, and then
they close. You try to reach for
the spaces between, even if most
of the time you come up empty.
But that's okay too, because it's
the trying that keeps you going.

DUMB MUMMIES

In these socially distanced Covid days
I stay mostly at home. I rifle through
bundles of old letters going back for
more than half a century. In our email-
and social-media-connected world hardly
anybody writes letters anymore.

But in those distant days they were
the lifeblood of long-distance
relationships: family, friends, lovers
and even some strangers now we
can't quite recall. These bundled epistles
smell musty and stale. Some have
yellowing ragged edges eating into
written words. They're pieces or shards
of past selves, flakes of skin of who
we once were or maybe hoped to be,
scarecrows now in the elongating
corridor of a faraway and dim past,
dumb mummies embalmed
in fading cursive, *memento mori*
of the lives we once lived.

FILLING UP THE CRY

"I do follow here in the chase, not like a hound that hunts,
but one that fills up the cry." [*Othello*]

It seemed to him that his whole life long
he ran with the pack, not as a lead dog
but only one of many to fill up the cry.
He didn't stand out; he only fitted in.

But as the years and decades went by
and the pack slowly thinned out as more
and more hounds fell by the wayside,
there he was, one of only a few hearty
hunters still running, nose still keen
on the scent of the game always
just beyond his sight or ken.

DYING BUTTERFLY

There it was at my feet: such
a tiny white thing in the grass
feebly flapping its fragile wings,
a mere smidgen against the green.
I sensed it was making a futile
dying effort, but I also sensed
that somehow we were part
and parcel of some greater
and all-pervading life force.

Illusion as that may be, and hope
against hope, thinking it might be
held down by a blade or two of grass,
I gingerly lifted it up to see if
it might still be able somehow
to take flight. Instead it dropped
from my hand straight down to
the ground, with not even a
quivering of its wings. So final
and so still it lay there that my
very mind seemed to reel as
I bowed my head in silence.

WHAT LASTS

Not you and I, but the stones we
step on in our walk in the woods.
The very wind in the trees sings the song
of our transience, as does the water
flowing down the gully. Words,
like those ancient stone pyramids,
last—so long as they're spoken
by someone even if not by us.

But what lasts the longest is
our dreams long after we're
gone and done, dreams that know
no generations but serve as
the fundament and bedrock
of all the passing human lives.

ALL AND NOTHING

Sometimes on a dismal rainy day like
this, I think that the longer we live
the less we learn. The whole world
seems like a huge flat tire,
and my daily quota or quotient
of experience nothing but
stale bread. It's then I suspect
that I may have outlived my days.

But then on the most rare of
rare occasions the coruscated
cataract film of ingrained
familiarity falls from my eyes
as I see the astonishing and
stunning miracle of a single flower.

And it's then that in the split of
a single second I catch a glimpse
of the perennial and abiding
mystery of All and Nothing.

Ephemeral Effusions of an Aging Brain During Pandemic Times

OLD AGE

The years whir by faster,
like the passing poles seen from
the window of a moving train.
Old memories turn from color
to a fading black and white.
.
Our faces don't seem to keep
their familiar shapes. Some
days we even become strangers
to ourselves, dropping in for
an unexpected and unwelcome
visit. When we look back on
the paths we've traveled over
the decades, the landscape
dematerializes and defamiliarizes.

When we try to look forward
we don't quite know where to look
or even what we're looking for.

Old friends now long gone
are a ghost gallery haunting
our uneasy dreams, or a
wax museum we do and
do not want to visit. The price
of admission is far too steep,
and the entryway is barred.

Sometimes the music of our
many years seems a mere
monotone, and the color
of our passing lives nothing
but a drab monochrome.

Sometimes the passing years
appear like a parade in which
we have to march, but nobody
ever salutes or cheers.

THE INFAMY OF REJECTION

If you want to know about the long-term
trials of rejection, dejection, abjection and
more, try to be a published poet. This stuff
is not for amateurs, but those only
who are in it for the longest of long hauls,
fighting day in and day out against
doors that always close just as you
try to approach them. Getting into
Kafka's Castle is a piece of cake
by comparison, a mere trifle. You pay
and you pay to enter a lottery you've
come to accept you can never ever win.

But you keep on playing Blind Man's
Buff because rejection is something
of which you can never get quite
enough. You've been a pro at it
for so very long that it simply seems
the order of the day. It's been part
of who and what you are that
will never go away so long as
you're around.

            Perpetual rejection
is the reward for those who
can grin and bear it, and who

wear it as a gold ribbon earned
in the futile race their hearts
have been pounding to all these
frivolous and futile wasted years.
It's a badge that proves you've
risen to the occasion every single
day even if you knew you were
playing all along in a losing game.

Year in, year out you've relentlessly
persisted. Yes, you've carried on and on,
and that, such as it is, my friend,
is your one and only claim to fame.

ROBERT FROST'S POETRY REJECTION LETTER

Dear Robert,

Thanks for submitting your two poems to the *Boston Literary Review*. We appreciate your sending them to us but regret to say that we are unable to make use of them at this time. Because you are clearly an amateur poet, we thought you might find some editorial suggestions helpful as you consider revising these poems and for others you may attempt to write. We suggest that you avoid the simple or simplistic rhymes you employ in both poems, and that you go for more verbal and sonic nuance: Contemporary poetry mostly eschews such namby-pamby triple rhymes as: know/though/snow, queer/near/year, shake/mistake/flake, deep/keep/sleep in "Stopping by Woods on a Snowy Evening." You repeat the same simplistic pattern in "The Road Not Taken": wood/stood/could, fair/wear/there. Lay/day/way, sigh/by/I. Try to be less repetitive and even metronomic, and strive for more variety if you must use rhymes. As for the content of these poems, we find your pose as a rural philosopher deep in thought in the first poem a bit jejune and quite unconvincing. Your diction and imagery too are rather trite—"downy flake," for instance, is what Wordsworth already dismissed as poetic diction at the end of the eighteenth century. And the repetition of the same line at the end of "Stopping by Woods" is overdone as a kind of concluding faux folksiness. Unfortunately, the same is true in "The Road Not Taken." The alternative of the two roads allows for no poetic nuance whatever. The "long I stood" is tedious phrasing, and the "Oh, I kept the first for another day!" is doubly offensive with the use of the archaic "oh" and then the exclamation point that is also a no-no in contemporary poetry. We suggest you familiarize yourself with the range of such contemporary poetry regularly featured in journals such as ours, and that may make all the difference in helping you to write the kind of sophisticated poetry produced by our best American poets today, and that doesn't put readers to sleep with bland rhymes and cliché sentiments. If you take these editorial suggestions in the positive spirit in which they are intended and seek to implement them into your future poetry writing efforts, we will be happy to consider a further submission from you.

Best wishes,

James Snarky, Editor

THE LONG NIGHT

We've been suffering through a long dark night
of the dead and the dying, but we also
know that dawn will come again with its
rosy fingers to announce the rising sun
with its brilliant multitudes of light.

After a long dark night the sun will rise.
The dying will not cease, but dawn will
come as it always does, and the sun
will rise: It will rise and rise day
after dawning day, to greet our hungry
eyes with all its miracles of light.

POETS ARE A DIME A DOZEN

I used to think poets imbibed an elixir
from some heavenly sphere,
and that everyone knew they were
among the chosen few,
the cream of the cream,
the icing on the cake
in this terrestrial scene:
but now I've come to know
poets merely are a dime a dozen.

I used to think that in the bustle and buzz
of the marketplace they occupied
a special place. Lawyers and judges
and politicians and such work behind
closed doors, but poets I thought
could not be bought and were
unacknowledged legislators
holding forth in the open air.

But now I know that here below
they're just a dime a dozen.
They don't bring us manna
from the skies, but mostly
Mavius-Bavius lies, and for
good cheer, mostly stale
flat beer that brings no
great joy to the hoi-polloi.

Poets aren't angelic messengers,
but merely fellow passengers on a ship
in storm-tossed seas. They aren't
spirits rarefied or refined,
they're just part of the unrefined
dross of ordinary humankind.

Once I thought they were among
the elect and the chosen,
but now I've come to know
they merely come a dime a dozen.

WOULDN'T IT BE NICE

Wouldn't it be nice if we could just get him
out of our minds? He's like an unwanted
relative who's come to visit
uninvited, and who won't leave
despite the biggest hints you can drop.
Wouldn't it be nice if in a trice
we could turn him out and not
have to see or hear him anymore?

And wouldn't it be nice if three
weeks from now his massive
rump will have definitively
been thumped, oh wouldn't
that just be so very sweet indeed?

He's taken up residence in our heads
like a visitor from Hell, and
and there's no chance we can
ever feel well again until he's sent
packing. He's so very full of himself,
braying and shouting, a very plague
upon the land, a fake Fuehrer
refusing to leave.

Wouldn't
it be so nice if we could finally
restore our minds to what they were
before he descended on our brains
like a disease without a cure?

Oh wouldn't it be ever so nice
If we could make him leave to
hunker down in his huge Bunker
of an Ego? Wouldn't it be just
wonderfully and refreshingly
nice for sure if we could just
kick him right out of our heads
and show him the door?

ZARATHUSTRA'S RETURN

After nearly a century and a half
Zarathustra departed his mountain
cave. His eagle and his serpent
he left behind him up there on
the heights. He hiked the trail down
to the valley below. Near the bottom
stood a little girl who seemed to be
waiting for him. As he approached
her, he saw she was holding a flower.
Her dress was blue, her eyes were
blue, and the flower was too. She
held it up to him by way of a
greeting, and he took it gladly.

But when he wanted to thank her,
he discovered that he could not
utter a single word. Not having spoken
for so very long, he found he'd lost
the gift of tongues. All he could do
was smile and nod, speechless.
She smiled back, and he went
on his solitary way, holding the
blue flower in his ancient hands.

ZARATHUSTRA IN THE VILLAGE

When Zarathustra entered the village
down in the valley he saw
an assembled multitude listening
to an animated speaker: It was
the latest face of demagoguery,
a member of the AFD or
Alternative for Germany
holding forth for all to hear and see.

The crowd, by now a seething mob,
inflamed by the orator's invectives
against the country's enemies,
hung on every word of his,
and shouted the slogans he fed
them, whose gist was to make
Germany great again, and to show
migrants and refugees the door
and make the country what it had been
once before. Only a few solitary
figures stood aside, and some
of them even look as if they cried.

Zarathustra didn't stay to hear
any more: he threw down
his blue flower in disgust,
and went on his way,
because he knew he must.

ZARATHUSTRA'S SONG

Zarathustra spent his first night
in the valley below in the hollow
of a tree. He knew that before
he could venture on human speech
he would have to sing to the wolves.

So Zarathustra sang the long-held
sorrow of his ancient soul in
the wide-spread silence of the night.
And the wolves came and squatted
in a circle on their haunches
around the tree, and their teeth
and eyes reflected the moonlight.

In the very stillness of the night
he sang his solitary song, and
the wolves sat and listened
mesmerized with their gleaming eyes.

THE UNIVERSE IS

Indifferent.
It doesn't bend
toward justice.
It doesn't bend
toward injustice.
It doesn't love.
It doesn't hate.
Only we love,
and only we hate.

The universe doesn't
mean anything in particular.
Only we do.
We mean to mean
and we do.
The Universe is
indifferent.

The Universe is.

WORDSWORTH TRIBUTE

William Wordsworth's greatest and most
enduring achievement as a philosophical
and visionary poet was his profound
insight into and passionate championing
of the inherent creativity of the human
mind and its myriad and mysterious
connections with the material world
to which it is exquisitely attuned:
the main haunt and region of his song.
Wordsworth was well worth his words

and then some.

THE INWARD PATH

"We dream of journeys through the universe.
But isn't the universe within us?"

[Novalis]

Researchers have recently found to their amazement
that the structure of the universe and that
of the human brain are essentially similar
if not the same: the patterns of billions
of stars and neurons share a common
configuration. Perhaps that's what Novalis
meant when he claimed that the mysterious
path leads inward, because the cosmos
is within us, and all it contains,
both past and future. And perhaps
the present moment is only
and always simply the fulcrum
of an unfathomable infinitude.

NOVEMBER 1, 2020

Today the leaves are blowing every which way.
There's snow in the forecast for tonight.
I haven't gotten around to resetting my watch
for daylight savings time, especially when
it seems I already have too much time
on my hands. And autumn is past its
prime, with winter waiting in the wings
to pounce. Maybe global warming will keep
it at bay, or at least allow for a delay.

Two days from now is the long-awaited
presidential election, as the nation
holds its breath. Whatever happens
and whoever wins, we know that
there's no way we can settle back
into the lives that we once knew.

Covid-19 has made quite sure of that.
The second wave—or is it the third?—
has not yet reached its raging peak,
and most of us know only too well
that we need to hunker down for now
and wait it out like a hurricane
that doesn't seem to want to end.

ELECTION DAY [NOVEMBER 3, 2020]

All we can do now is hold our collective breath.
Twelve years ago at the end of this day
I wrote that the wheel of history had
turned when Obama was elected.
I was so very hopeful then.

But now this nation is so divided
that the pursuit of a common
good seems like a mere mirage.
The pandemic is raging increasingly
out of control and a self-promoting
blustering and bullying fraud may
win. I hope not, but hope is always
a fragile thing at best, a paper
airplane in the wind, or
a child's simple prayer.

NOVEMBER 26, 2020

The sun's watery eye filters through
layers of clouds. The goldenrods so
resplendent in September now wave
their grey-slivered heads in the wind.

There's much to be thankful for even
in these days of a pandemic surging
across the nation. It's a mild day
today, before the winter cold sets
in this coming week. And the
buffoon-in-chief will be out
of office in less than two months.

That's something to be grateful for,
even though the death toll he
tried to ignore so ostrich-like
is now approaching three hundred
thousand and will continue to
grow until it peaks. For now
we keep our fingers firmly
crossed in expectation of
the better times ahead.

ZARATHUSTRA'S NIGHT VIGIL

"And many a one who turned away from life, turned away only from the riff-raff: he did not wish to share fountain, flame, or fruit with that riff-raff."

—Nietzsche, *Thus Spake Zarathustra*

Like the insurgent Nazarene preacher's poor,
the riffraff will always be with us,
trumpeting and trumpeting and trumpeting
their lowlife ways. They are the loudest
voices of our passing days. They are
the empty noise of the world sounding
ad nauseam until our ears grow deaf
from fear of having to hear them
again and again and again.

Here
in my retreat up in the hills I can
almost block them out, almost,
yes, but not quite: the empty blather
of the world and the Idiot Wind that
Zarathustra chose to rise above
by going up into the high mountains
and observing the inane doings
of the demented world below
with eagle eyes and a serpent's
cunning, leaving Plato's dark cave

to the teeming legions of this forever
fallen and irredeemable world.

High up there on those snow-covered
alpine heights Zarathustra sat
silent during those crystal clear nights,
entranced by the glittering stars
and galaxies he did not have to share
with the trumpeting herds below.

And during those long hours of
his protracted vigil the thought
of fountain, fruit, and flame
calmed his troubled mind.

INDIGLO

Late at night as I lie awake
I like to run my fingers over
the smooth crystal surface
of my Timex Indiglo watch.

It's almost as if I can feel
the very flow of time,
and with it the perpetual
passing of my life. Somehow
that smooth surface is reassuring,
the warm feel and face of time
on my fingertips invisible
until I press the button
on the side of the watch,
and the precise hours and
minutes light up in a golden
glow in the surrounding dark.

Time may be an invisible arrow,
but for me it lights up at night.

WINTER SOLSTICE, DECEMBER 21, 2020

Tonight will be the longest dark night
of a long and mostly dreary dark year:
A global pandemic and disaster-prone
time with a dizzying and mounting
death toll in which most of us learned
to walk abroad masked, but some
stubbornly refused, helping to spread
the virulent virus among family,
friends, and even random others.

Dawn's first gleams of this longest
night that is also a great divide
will usher in a new season
of shorter nights and longer
days, as well as a new year when
the dying will peak only to decline
as the vaccine becomes more
and more available to all,
and when so much death
and dying will have opened our
eyes and minds to the possibilities
of a new year and even a new
world when shaken to our core
we learn to embrace the gathering
light after this protracted
dark night: a year when we can

meet again with family, friends,
and strangers to recognize,
affirm, and celebrate anew our
resurgent and indestructible humanity.

POĖTE MAUDIT DOGGEREL

Je suis comme on dit
un poète maudit
always barking up the wrong tree.

A poet marginal as well
as anyone with a tuppence
worth of brains can tell.
And a Hungerkünstler too
asleep in the straw in the
sideshow of a traveling zoo
in a world that grows stranger
too by the day while the
politicians and the Wall Street
hucksters and hedge fund
managers make hay.

A poète maudit, it's true,
but one who can see right through
the tsunamis of corruption
that are the order of the day.
Yes, toujours du jour.

TAIL END [DECEMBER 25, 2020]

Here at the tail end of a disastrous
year it's a quiet Christmas Day.
Rain during the night turned
to snow with enough cover
for a White Christmas I didn't
even bother dreaming about
during these resurgent and
escalating Covid-19 days,
with people traveling by the
millions for family gatherings
despite the warnings of public
officials and medical experts.

People will do what people
will do, even at the peril of
their and many others' lives.
Well over three hundred thousand
dead and counting. But here
at the tail end of this
disease-blighted year we
look in the direction of a
new year in which the double
disasters of Trump and
Covid will be well in our
collective rearview mirror.

Here, at the tail end of
this unbelievable year.

SIREN SONGS

I don't need anyone to tie me to the mast
of the ship or seal my ears with wax
so I can't hear the fabled sea-singing
of the Sirens. I want to hear them
with my ears and eyes wide open.

I'm willing to take that risk, whatever
it may entail, and hazard the open seas
to catch a fleeting glimpse of those ancient
creatures singing in unison to lure
sailors to their shipwrecked doom.

To be folded into the swell and surge
of those rapturous sounds in an
ecstatic embrace and sink down into
the infinite sea would be a better fate
by far than to sit becalmed on
shore sipping the dregs in of a
pedestrian life, and nothing more.

WILL THE SHADOWS THAT HAVE BATTENED ON US

Will the shadows that have battened on us in the old year
continue to prey on us in the new one, to confound
us to the core as a nation and call into question
who and what we are at our best and our worst?

Will the voices of ignorance, bigotry, and downright
delusion prevail as the new order of the day?
Will the rational and those of good will be able
to have their say and push back against the
tide of lunacy by the besotted sloganeering
herd? Can sanity and decency still stand up to
and prevail against the onslaught of mounting
and ingrained prevarications? Will the boldfaced
chorus of lies continue to set the tone and be
the tune to which those enamored of them
will march? What resource or safeguard is left
to the decent and the true short of sheer despair?
What hope against dark hearts set on undoing
the very web and woof of the nation's integrity?

But we know that whatever may come our way
the sun will continue to rise and set, that
spring will come and the crocuses push
through the melting snow; we know that in May
the daffodils will blow in the wind,
resplendent in their prime, and we know

that children will continue to take in the wonder
and magic of the world with wide-open eyes.

We know too that ancient truths known
and honored since times immemorial
have no expiration date but will continue
to fuel the fire in the hearts of those who
stay true to what is right and good and
who know how to steer a steady course
no matter what strong storm winds may blow.

FOR MARK AND HELEN TOCHEN

We discover that our happiness depends
especially in our later years on good old friends.
Old friends are like those finely seasoned wines
in whose taste the splendor of our years shines.
Standing out among such friends are Mark and Helen
whose kindness over the years is beyond telling.
As we grow old and older who and what we are
shines with the dim radiance of a distant star.
We can't always see that light due to clouds
that sometimes cover the sky like a host of shrouds.
But we always know that light is still there
as clear as ever and ready to share
the rhythms of our joys as well as our sorrows
as we face the uncertain prospect of our tomorrows.

THE FERMI PARADOX QUESTION

It's a perplexing question for sure
that Fermi famously asked several
decades ago: so where is everybody?
In a galaxy of over one hundred
billion stars there have to be
intelligent beings spread around
wide and far. And our Milky Way is
only one of billions of galaxies!

So how come we haven't been contacted
or detected anything to show that
we're not the only intelligent species
in this vast universe? Surely that would
be the greatest miracle of all!

Or are there alien species out there
so unimaginably far evolved beyond
us that they can see and hear us without
our knowing? That they can overleap
space and time and the speed of
light limit? And that they haven't
made themselves known to us
because we're still so primitive that
we're not even worth the bother?

INVISIBLE DOOR

"I define surveillance capitalism as the unilateral claiming of private human experience as free raw material for translation into behavioral data. These data are then computed and packaged as prediction products and sold into behavioral futures markets—business customers with a commercial interest in knowing what we will do now, soon, and later."—Shoshana Zuboff

One day you walk through an invisible door
and suddenly you don't recognize your old
familiar world anymore. It's as if you're suddenly
snow-blind, only there's no snow anywhere.
Invisible networks you've never even known
are now the new order of the day. The world
you knew and counted on is now forever gone.

You can't walk back to who or where or what
you once were. Neither can you stay in place as
you face these new and unfamiliar exigencies.
The old world has taken leave of you, or
you of it, and you don't even know which
is which. The only thing you can do in your
perplexed befuddlement is negotiate with
the onslaught of the new to see that even
if there can't be a reprieve, a truce might
somehow be arranged for you to come to
terms with the onslaught of the unfamiliar,
the unyielding, and the strange.

"BABY, BABY, BABY, YOU'RE OUT OF TIME"

Mick Jagger, back in his prime, sang it
about a girl who rejected him, but I take
it as a telling existential theme for where
we've been in these pandemic times now
for a year or more. Out of time: some
folks have too much time on their hands, some
too little, and some in the ICU on ventilators
just about none. To some it seems as if
they're adrift on a boat in the sea with
no prospect of any rescue.

Out of time may
mean days that are blank pages in an
encyclopedia of countless volumes
in an epic library. Time is and time
was and time that will be are an
incomprehensible history of arrested
lives in an apparent perpetual stasis.
Lives of quarantined plans and
schemes where the relentless ticking
of a covert clock is the measured
metronome of such suspended
moments stretched out to infinity,
uncounted, unnumbered, and
forever out of time.

ICICLE

Curious it is how the mind metaphorizes.
Out of my study window on this late
February morning I observe a very
long icicle hanging off the edge
of the roof gutter where it had been
growing for days, and now it's about
three feet long, shaped like a spear,
from whose tip water drops fall—
yesterday one every three seconds
or so with great regularity, but this
morning one right after the
other, in an unremitting cascade.

And so my mind took a metaphoric
turn. I couldn't help but see that
accelerating parade of water drops
from the pointed icicle spear tip as
an image of our lives speeding up
and relentlessly by in our later years.

STATUES

"'Tis time. Descend. Be stone no more. Approach."

In a Shakespeare play a stone statue
becomes living flesh once more.

In the world I live in now I can see
that so many of my contemporaries
have turned into statues, their living
flesh cold as stone, their hearts
granite hard. Frozen in time
they seem to stand stock-
still. What ideas they once
had have hardened into solid
rock. Unmoved so many
now stand by the suffering
and the evil in our world.

Do awake your faith
was the preamble and
injunction to make that
statue move and embrace
her life again. To awake
our faith is indeed the great
challenge of these our dismal
times to make those rock-
hardened hearts beat
to the very beat of human

kindness, compassion,
and genuine deep caring.

If only we could do so
and awake our faith in
this so fallen and fractured
world and make those myriad
many statues among us
be stone no more and
move to the best music
that is or should be at
the eternal core of our
essential human being.

THE GRAVITY OF DREAMS

We look to the future as the event horizon
of our lives. And rightly so, for that's
where our lives will continue to play
out in ways we can only dream about
without being able to exactly script
them according to a certain calculus.

The future always beckons to us in
not quite discernible forms. But
sometimes it's our nightly dreams
that want to draw us back into the lives
that we've already lived, and do so
in distorted and barely recognizable
shapes. Like gravity does our bodies,
they draw us back to who or what
we once were, to selves we think
we've outlived or overcome, like
old clothes we outgrew so long ago.

WHAT THE TREES KNOW

The thing about trees is that they know
how to stand their ground, unless we cut
them down or fierce storms uproot them.
The deep-anchored ancient ones have a wisdom
we can't begin to comprehend or aspire to,
they who can outlive us by generations
and more. They are the door to a world
we have forever lost, though we no longer
even know that. They can make the wind
sing and the sun dance when it dapples
their leaves in great profusion, these veterans
of the perennially passing years. Trees
have their own reasons for being who
and what they are and have always been.

They can even sense where we are headed,
though that's a hidden leaf knowledge
they choose to keep strictly to themselves.
What we have forgotten long ago they
know how to preserve, season after season.

WHERE DO POEMS COME FROM?

Sometimes when you're far from home you meet
and greet them like old friends you've never known.
Sometimes they are the silky stardust sifting though
your fingers. Sometimes in a long sleepless night
you stumble over one in the dark hallway and
then you thank it for being there so out of sight.
And sometimes they're the first glimmer
of dawn, a glorious ray piercing the dark.

All the poems that can ever be written
already exist in the hyperspace of the human
brain, and all you need is the great and good
fortune to suddenly be able to pull one down
after years of practice like a ripe and luscious
fruit. And sometimes poems simply come utterly
unsought out of nowhere and if you're lucky
enough to be there at the right moment
you can catch one like a fish in a stream
with your wide open and waiting bare hands.

CAROUSEL OF THE SEASONS

If the round of the seasons is a merry-go-round,
it's one that never stops—and there's only one
way to get off it. Like the V-shaped gaggle of geese
we see and hear honking in early November skies
there are those who know how to cheat the seasons
by heading south, human snowbirds seeking warmer
climes. But we stay here with the perennial round that
seems to keep on getting shorter as we get older.

Round and round we go: Spaceship earth spins
on its axis every twenty-four hours, and
completes its circuit of the sun once a year.
We ride on the carousel of the cycling seasons,
travelers and passengers of the revolving years,
always headed back to where we've already
been so many times before in an immense
ocean of space and time without any shore.

NO FLOWER METAPHOR

I don't really know my way around flowers,
though off the top of my head I can list the names
of some: roses, carnations, irises, daffodils,
daisies, orchids, tulips, chrysanthemums.

That pretty much covers it. Being Dutch,
my wife likes tulips, save that in a vase they
only last a short time. She prefers alstroemerias,
because when you get them really fresh
they can last up to a couple of weeks.
Her favorite ones are purple. We have
a large bunch of these sitting on the glass-
topped living room table. They've
been there for over ten days, and
yesterday morning I found a single
petal on the glass, looking forlorn,
and this morning yet another. I picked
each one up carefully so as not to
smudge the tabletop, and deposited
them in the trash. I know more will start
dropping each day, and it won't be long
until this purple bunch too will be history.

In my mind's eye I can see a cascade
of falling petals, but I resolutely refuse
the temptation to turn that thought

into a mere metaphor. Flowers are
both too real and exquisitely fragile
for that. But then flowers always fade,
unlike metaphors that have
no expiration date.

MAGIC

They say that magic doesn't happen
in real life. But I say that maybe it does
and we just don't see it. We're blind to it
save for the rarest of occasions, and then
when it does we write it off with our rational
minds as a fluke, the sooner forgotten,
the better. Children sometimes do see it,
but they lack the words to capture it.
And if we do catch a glimpse of a
magical moment we shudder
and shut our eyes.

Magical moments are like butterflies
that silently flutter by as we stick
our heads in the sand and smugly
take comfort in how rational and
even wise we think we really are.

But then reality stretches far, far
beyond our so routinely circumscribed
ken. Magic is like when the first green
shoots of spring appear that we simply
take for granted and casually pass by.

PROFESSOR OF RETIREMENT

I have time to read the *NY Times* front
to back, not that I'm any the wiser for
it. I have the time for two long dog walks
a day and doubles tennis several times
a week. I have time for lazy afternoon
naps and several evening news programs
and then more television viewing after
that. I have time to read books and forget
most of what's in them soon after because
I know that I don't have to teach them.
My teaching days are done and then some,
so now I read strictly for diversion.

Diversion from what? The increasingly
precarious state of the world, plague plagued,
globally warming, fanatical factions at
each other's throats the world over,
the very world the first astronauts on
the moon saw as a beautiful but fragile
blue and white balloon suspended in empty
space, so very exquisite and inexplicable
that miraculous and ever-shrinking
globe on which we live so much at odds
with each other so much of the time.

Diversion also from the pressing thought
of my mortality that bears down on me
like gravity, the grave thought of the grave
that's the half-hidden script of retirement,
the fatal killjoy that makes the precious
remaining moments and days sparkle
like raindrops in the sun or the rising
fizz of a newly poured glass of champagne.

CLICHÉ PEARLS OF FAUX WISDOM

Talk is cheap, but I've told you time and again
that because not all roads lead to Rome
I took a busman's holiday to carry coals
to Newcastle to see what I could see.
I never upset the apple cart, because
I know that the apple doesn't fall far
from the tree. An apple a day will keep
the doctor away, and what doesn't kill
us makes us stronger. A penny saved is
a penny earned. So in for a penny,
in for a pound. After all, beggars
can't be choosers. That, my friends,
is the long and the short of it. I know
that all good things come to him who
waits, even if they sometimes come
a tad too late. We know that history
repeats itself, so do give credit where
credit is due, for great minds always
think alike. Boys will be boys, even
though blood is thicker than water.
Then again a dog is a man's best friend,
and misery loves company. So don't
cast your pearls before swine or
ever judge a book by its cover. And
if familiarity breeds contempt,
remember that walls have ears.

Even if ignorance isn't always bliss,
don't look a gift horse in the mouth
because bad news travels fast and
actions always speak louder than words.
Let's face it: it is what it is because
a fool and his money are easily parted.
So count your blessings, because
curiosity killed the cat. Seeing is
believing, for stupid is as stupid
does. But I'm preaching to the choir,
so, ready or not, the die is cast:
tomorrow is just another day and
where there's a will there's always
a way. You are what you eat, so
never say never because you're never
too old to learn and you don't tell
tales out of school. No pain, no gain.
Loose lips sink ships, but a rising tide
lifts all boats. No news is good news
and practice makes perfect.

THE SUPREME COURT AND THE ARTICLE "A"

A response to "A Sharp Divide at the Supreme Court
Over a One-Letter Word" [*NY Times*, May 1, 2021]

When the nine Supreme Court Justices can't agree
on the meaning of the simple article "A,"
how can we possibly trust what they have to say
about what the words in the Constitution meant then
or even what they might mean today?

"A" is the simplest of simple words we use every day,
but if these highly honed legal minds can't agree
what it means in a document before them, how can we
trust their ability to see judiciously and correctly
into the soul of the Constitution as a complex whole?

If those sage Nine can't reach a consensus to define
the meaning of a simple letter, what better chance
can they have with the Constitution's Articles and the Clauses
which must give them dizzying interpretive pauses
in their black-robed rigmarole of a judicial dance?
When the nine Justices can't agree on the meaning of "A"
all the rest of us can do is close our eyes and pray.

BOB DYLAN TURNS EIGHTY [MAY 24, 2021]

Today Robert Allen Zimmerman, aka Bob Dylan,
turned eighty. The times they have a-changed
time after time, but we who are older if not
wiser also know only too well that in some fashion
they also always stay ultimately the same. Who
and what we once were in those music blasting
song-rich and riotous 1960s has turned to
smoke-rings in our minds, and only the Idiot
Wind has not changed its tune. The Ghost of
Electricity is still heading West on a train,
and cries just like a woman. We're far older
now, but *may you stay forever young* is the
most beautiful of his wishes or benedictions,
a blessing we seek to grasp like a Platonic
idea that always eludes our grasp. We were
so much younger then, but we know
that his oh so many songs will serve as an
inspiration and a source of visionary
insight for many generations to come,
even in a fallen world replete with murders
most foul, fueled by the profiteering
Masters of War that he called out so
boldly some seven decades ago.

Oh Baby

Blue, you who were such a true and
inspirational voice for us when we were
still youth-green, when that magical swirling
ship comes sailing to take you away as it
inevitably must, may your chameleon soul
embrace it as yet another stage in the
endless journey of your song-poetry's so
long-lived and celebrated career.

MID-JUNE MASSACRE

We walk the trails in our woods to the sound
of something that sounds like falling rain.
Shards and fragments of green leaves litter
the ground. What we hear falling isn't rain
drops but the millions of caterpillar gipsy
moths ravaging and savaging the late
spring foliage, despoiling the trees.

They will feast for several more weeks
before this year's leaf massacre ends.
We can only hope the trees will survive
to face another onslaught next year,
the third and last of this relentless plague.

Hearing the seemingly unceasing
barrage as we walk under the trees,
I realize I can't really curse this
horde of caterpillar moths because
it brings home to us that everything
that lives ultimately always does
so at the expense of something or
somebody else, and that the strict
economy of nature is based on
such unceasing predation.

At least here walking in our woods
we know what is preying on what,
unlike in the greater world out
there, where predators too often
pose as benevolent benefactors.

THE GREATEST WONDER

The philosopher Kant famously asserted
that there were two things that filled him
with awe: the starry heavens above,
and the moral law within him.

It seems that for most humans most
of the time that law is pretty dim—
and when observed, then more in
preaching than in actual practice.

As for those multitudes of stars,
they are an infinitely layered record
of the billennial past of our universe.
That starry firmament is a ghost
gallery that fills us with wonder.

What may well be the greatest wonder
of all is the human brain that has begun
to decipher this great mystery but that
for the most part we simply take for
granted, as if it weren't the abiding
miracle it so obviously and amazingly is.

EPHEMERAL

Ephemeral: transitory, lasting only a day.
So says my dictionary. I think
of my poems like that. They're
like clouds that drift by in the sky,
and then they're gone. Like our
days that drift by, and nobody
knows for sure exactly how or
why. Like our lives, whether
short- or long-lived.

So what I do is a simple kind of
sky writing as my phrases soar
through the air wrapped in a
thin white mist. *Ephemeral.*
Transitory. Lasting only a day.

Merely passing effusions of my
wayward and wandering thoughts.
Just saying.

ONCE, OR ONCE AGAIN?

Rilke said, each one of us *once,*
and once only. But earlier Nietzsche
insisted on the Eternal Return. All that's
ever happened will happen again.
I'm not sure whether he saw
this as a good or a bad scenario—
I guess I read him too long ago.

For instance, could the horrors of the
Holocaust really be repeated again?
A dreadful thought for sure, but we've
had plenty of proof since that it could
happen once more, even if so far not
yet on the same scale of sheer human
monstrosity. In light of that, I can't
help but think that Rilke's *once, and*
once only must be the best way to go.
Yes, maybe once and only once is
more than enough for us here below.

MAUSOLEUM, OR THE OTHER SIDE OF LIFE [ON THE OCCASION OF TURNING SEVENTY-EIGHT]

"trailing clouds of glory do we come"

On the other side of life things look different
than from when you first set out as a mere child.
On the other side of life dreams can become
the repository of who you once were that
you pay nocturnal visits to. The ghosts who
live there are merely the different selves you
once were or wore. Perhaps the moon's dark
side is a mausoleum rich in patterns of
chiaroscuro, or maybe a mere fading palette of
dim memories that follow you, the photographic
negatives of the long life you've somehow
managed to live through. No, not trailing clouds
of glory, on the other side of life the many
things you see in the dark mirrors of memory
do assume rich shades of endless ambiguity.

Riches that in the glorious poverty of who you
were when you first set out in a world that
grows stranger by the day you had not
the faintest clue would somehow accrue
in the fabulous reversion of your dreams here
on the dark side of the moon that is the
other side of life that so many never even
live long enough to live or breathe. The other

side is at once a mausoleum and the very
museum of all you've ever done and been,
and mysteriously enough, somehow come
to be. And cloudless skies are what,
hope against hope, you still hope to see.

ON THE OREGON COAST [JULY 2021]

As I walked along the shore of the sea,
what I thought I heard was the
thundering sound of eternity:
those *mighty waters rolling evermore.*

On the bare sands I picked up
a wet shell as a sand dollar token
of this seacoast epiphany about
the perpetual recurrence of
everything we ever hear or see.

And as I held the shell in my hand
I could almost hear my heart sing.

WAVES

Wave after wave has washed over me
in the course of a long life,
but I still stand with my feet
firmly planted on the shore
even though I don't know how
many more are still to come
before my life's long journey
is finally over with and done.
In the meantime I grit my teeth
and carry on. I'm more than
happy to embrace all those
waves I can still brave.

www.ingramcontent.com/pod-product-compliance
Lightning Source LLC
LaVergne TN
LVHW020527100826
845148LV00010B/1376
* 9 7 9 8 3 8 5 2 7 2 5 2 5 *